AQA
GCSE Mathematics
Modular

Sue Chandler   Ewart Smith

Foundation

Module 1

Series editor: Harry Smith
Consultant examiner: David Pritchard

STOKE PARK
SCHOOL & COMMUNITY TECHNOLOGY COLLEGE
DANE ROAD
COVENTRY CV2 4JW

www.heinemann.co.uk
✓ Free online support
✓ Useful weblinks
✓ 24 hour online ordering

01865 888058

Heinemann Educational Publishers
Halley Court, Jordan Hill, Oxford OX2 8EJ
Part of Harcourt Education

Heinneman is the registered trademark of Harcourt Education Limited

© Text Sue Chandler, Ewart Smith 2006

First published 2006

10 09 08 07 06
10 9 8 7 6 5 4 3 2 1

British Library Cataloguing in Publication Data is available from the British Library on request.

10-digit ISBN: 0 435807 19 6
13-digit ISBN: 978 0 435807 19 1

The right of Sue Chandler and Ewart Smith to be identified as joint authors of this book has been asserted by them in accordance with the Copyright, Designs and Patents Act 1988.

Copyright notice
All rights reserved. No part of this publication may be reproduced in any form or by any means (including photocopying or storing it in any medium by electronic means and whether or not transiently or incidentally to some other use of this publication) without the written permission of the copyright owner, except in accordance with the provisions of the Copyright, Designs and Patents Act 1988 or under the terms of a licence issued by the Copyright Licensing Agency, 90 Tottenham Court Road, London W1T 4LP. Applications for the copyright owner's written permission should be addressed to the publisher.

Edited by Carol Harris
Designed by Wooden Ark Studios
Typeset by Tech-Set Ltd, Gateshead, Tyne and Wear

Original illustrations © Harcourt Education Limited, 2006
Illustrated by Dylan Gibson
Cover design by mccdesign
Printed in United Kingdom by Scotprint

Cover photo: Getty Images/Digital Vision©
Consultant examiners: David Pritchard, Andy Darbourne
Series editor: Harry Smith

Acknowledgements
Harcourt Education Ltd would like to thank those schools who helped in the development and trialling of this course.

The author and publisher would like to thank the following individuals and organisations for permission to reproduce photographs:

Alamy Images pp **5, 10, 62**; Corbis pp **7, 45, 96, 97**;
Getty Images/PhotoDisc pp **16, 19, 46, 72, 117** (top); Harcourt Education Ltd/Phil Bratt pp **18**;
Getty Images/Image Bank pp **48**; Harcourt Education Ltd/Mark Bassett pp **53**;
Harcourt Education Ltd/Debbie Rowe pp **68**; iStock Photo pp **113**;
Harcourt Education Ltd/Arnos Design pp **117**; Digital Vision pp **38**.

Every effort has been made to contact copyright holders of material reproduced in this book. Any omissions will be rectified in subsequent printings if notice is given to the publishers.

Publishing team

Editorial	Design/Production	Picture research
Sarah Flockhart	Christopher Howson	Chrissie Martin
Maggie Rumble	Phil Leafe	
Joanna Shock	Helen McCreath	

There are links to relevant websites in this book. In order to ensure that the links are up-to-date, that the links work, and that sites are not inadvertently linked to sites that could be considered offensive, we have made the links available on the Heinemann website at www.heinemann.co.uk/hotlinks. When you access the site, the express code is 7196P.

Tel: 01865 888058 www.heinemann.co.uk www.tigermaths.co.uk

How to use this book

This book is designed to give you the best possible preparation for your AQA GCSE Module 1 Examination. The authors are experienced writers of successful school mathematics textbooks and each book has been exactly tailored to your GCSE maths specification.

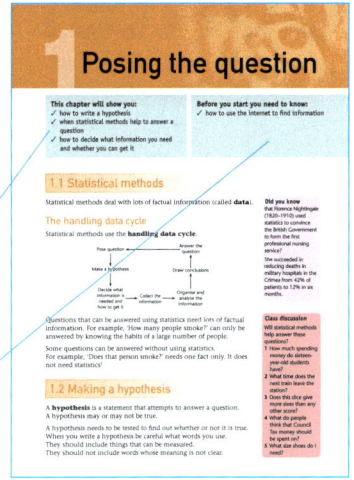

Finding your way around

To help you find your way around when you are studying and revising use the

- **contents list** – this gives a detailed breakdown of the topics covered in each chapter
- **list of objectives** at the start of each chapter – this tells you what you will learn in the chapter
- **list of prerequisite knowledge** at the start of each chapter – this tells you what you need to know before starting the chapter
- **index** – on page 151 – you can use this to find any topic covered in this book.

Remembering key facts

At the end of each chapter you will find

- **a summary of key points** – this lists the key facts and techniques covered in the chapter
- **grade descriptions** – these tell you which techniques and skills most students need to be able to use to achieve each exam grade
- **a glossary** – this gives the definitions of the mathematical words used in the chapter.

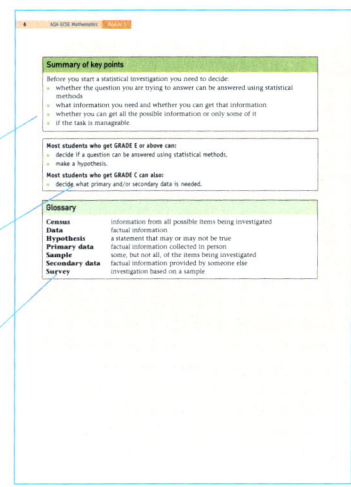

Exercises and practice papers

- **Worked examples** show you exactly how to answer exam questions.
- **Tips and hints** highlight key techniques and explain the reasons behind the answers.
- **Exam practice** questions work from the basics up to exam level. Hints and tips help you achieve your highest possible grade.
- **An examination practice paper** on page 129 helps you prepare for your written examination.
- **Answers** for all the questions are included at the end of the book.

Coursework, communication and technology

- **Mini coursework tasks** throughout the book will help you practice the skills needed for your GCSE coursework tasks.
- **ICT tasks** will highlight opportunities to use computer programs and the Internet to help your understanding of mathematical topics.
- **Class discussion** sections allow you to talk about problems and what techniques you might use to solve them.

Contents

MODULE 1 Foundation tier

1 Posing the question

Statistical methods	1
Making a hypothesis	1
Finding information	2
Manageability	4

2 Collecting data

Types of data	7
Data collection sheets	8
Designing a data collection sheet	9
Grouped data	11
Discrete and continuous data	13
Collecting related data	16
Sampling	18
Questionnaires	19

3 Representing data 1

Pictograms	23
Bar charts for ungrouped data	26
Drawing bar charts	29
Frequency polygons for ungrouped data	30
Frequency polygons for grouped data	33

4 Representing data 2

Pie charts	38
Drawing pie charts	41
Stem-and-leaf diagrams	43
Completing and drawing a stem-and-leaf diagram	45
Reading time-series graphs	48
Index numbers	52

5 Range and averages

Range	55
Mode	56
Median	57
Mean	59
Range, mode and median from frequency tables and diagrams	60
The mean from an ungrouped frequency table	64
Range, mode and median from grouped frequency tables	67
Finding the mean of a grouped frequency distribution	70

6 Two-way tables and scatter graphs

Two-way tables	75
Using and plotting scatter graphs	77
Line of best fit	80
Correlation	82

7 Probability 1

Probability	87
Outcomes of an experiment	87
The probability scale	88
Calculating probabilities	90
Events that can happen in more than one way	92
Using frequency diagrams	95
The number of times an event is likely to happen	96
Games of chance	98

8 Probability 2

Probability that an event does not happen	101
Mutually exclusive outcomes	103
Sample spaces	105
Using a sample space to find probabilities	108
Relative frequency	111

9 Conclusions

Drawing conclusions	116
Comparing data	120

Examination practice paper	129
Answers	138
Index	151

1 Posing the question

This chapter will show you:
- ✓ how to write a hypothesis
- ✓ when statistical methods help to answer a question
- ✓ how to decide what information you need and whether you can get it

Before you start you need to know:
- ✓ how to use the internet to find information

1.1 Statistical methods

Statistical methods deal with lots of factual information (called **data**).

The handling data cycle

Statistical methods use the **handling data cycle**.

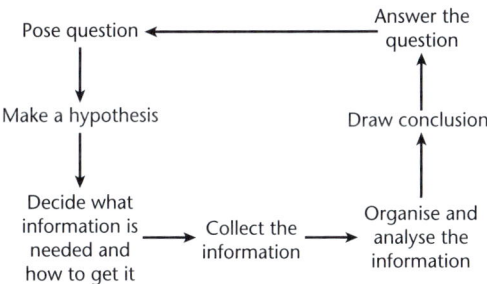

Questions that can be answered using statistics need lots of factual information. For example, 'How many people smoke?' can only be answered by knowing the habits of a large number of people.

Some questions can be answered without using statistics. For example, 'Does that person smoke?' needs one fact only. It does not need statistics!

1.2 Making a hypothesis

A **hypothesis** is a statement that attempts to answer a question. A hypothesis may or may not be true.

A hypothesis needs to be tested to find out whether or not it is true. When you write a hypothesis be careful what words you use. They should include things that can be measured. They should not include words whose meaning is not clear.

Did you know
that Florence Nightingale (1820–1910) used statistics to convince the British Government to form the first professional nursing service?

She succeeded in reducing deaths in military hospitals in the Crimea from 42% of patients to 12% in six months.

Class discussion
Will statistical methods help answer these questions?
1 How much spending money do sixteen-year-old students have?
2 What time does the next train leave the station?
3 Does this dice give more sixes than any other score?
4 What do people think that Council Tax money should be spent on?
5 What size shoes do I need?

Example 1

Write a hypothesis for the question 'Does smoking shorten life?'

Smoking more than 1 cigarette a day reduces life expectancy.

> This hypothesis has an exact meaning and can be tested.

Example 2

Give a reason why 'Smokers die young.' is not a good hypothesis.

'Smokers' means different things to different people.

> 'Young' can also mean different things to different people; 'five' is young to a twenty-year-old and 'fifty' is young to an eighty-year-old.

Exam practice 1A

A01

1. Amy wrote this hypothesis:

   Fat people die young.

   Write down **one** reason why this is not a good hypothesis to test.

   > 'Fat' is not clear enough to measure. You could use 'Clinically obese' which can be measured – it is a body mass index over 30.

2. Write down **one** reason why each of the following is not a good hypothesis to test.
   a Fit people do not become ill very often.
   b Young people have lost interest in politics.
   c More old people vote in a general election than young people.

A01

3. David asked 'If the price of alcohol is increased, will this stop people getting drunk?'
   a Write down a hypothesis for this question.
   b Give a reason why this might be difficult to test.

A01

> **Did you know**
> that you can find your body mass index by dividing your weight in kilograms by the square of your height in metres?

1.3 Finding information

The next step is to decide what information is needed and if you can get it. These questions help with your planning.
- What information is needed?
- Does the information exist?
- Can you get this information?

Primary and secondary data

There are two main sources of information – secondary data and primary data.

Secondary data is information that has already been collected.

You can get secondary data from several places. Newspapers, books and the Internet are good places to look.

Primary data is information you collect yourself.

You can get primary data by measuring, asking people questions or carrying out an experiment.

Class discussion

For each of the following hypotheses discuss what information is needed and how the information can be found.
1. Runner bean seeds germinate 2 weeks after they are planted.
2. Three-year-old cars are cheaper than one-year-old cars.
3. People who do not eat green vegetables have more days off work than those that do.
4. Most people do not pay all the tax that they should pay.
5. Self-employed people work longer hours and take shorter holidays than employed people.

Example 3

Max wants to test the hypothesis
'More people over 40 years old use their vote than younger people.'
Answer each of the following questions.
  a What information does Max need?
  b Does this information exist? Give a reason for your answer.
  c How can Max get this information?

  a Peoples' ages and when they have voted.
  b Yes. People know how old they are and most will know when they have voted.
  c Max could find some opinion polls that have this information.
     He may also be able find some information on the Internet.
     Max can collect the information himself by asking people questions.

Exam practice 1B

1. To test each of the following hypotheses, say whether you would need to collect primary or secondary data.
    a Year 11 students are faster runners than Year 7 students.
    b It is more likely to rain in Edinburgh than in Brighton.
    c Small cars are more fuel efficient than large cars.
    d Students in my class prefer maths lessons to English lessons.

2. Ellie wants to test the hypothesis:
   'Girls have faster reaction times than boys.'
    a What information does Ellie need?
    b How could Ellie get this information?

> **ICT task**
> Use a search engine on your computer to find websites giving information on:
> **a** Voting patterns by age.
> **b** Prices of secondhand cars.

1.4 Manageability

The manageability of a task is how easy or difficult it is to carry out.
- How much information do I need?
  The answer to this is always 'as much as possible.' But what is possible depends on what data you want. It also depends on the time available and the cost of collecting the data.
- Is this task manageable?
  Before you start to collect information, ask yourself these questions.
  'Do I have enough time to do this?'
  and 'Will it cost too much?'

Census or survey?

A **census** gives information on all of the things you are investigating.

If you want the heights of oak trees in a small wood, you can probably get all of them. This is a census.

A **sample** is some but not all the things you are investigating.
A **survey** is an investigation that uses a sample.

If you want the heights of oak trees in the UK, you will not be able to get them all. You will have to select some of them. The number that you select depends on the time you have available. Those that you select are the sample.

Exam practice 1C

1. Gerry is investigating the statement
   'Girls get better GCSE grades in maths than boys.'
   He uses a list of the grades from students in one school.
   Is Gerry doing a census or a survey?
   Explain your answer.

2. Kay is investigating the statement
   'This dice gives more sixes than it should.'
   She rolls the dice 100 times and writes down what it shows each time.
   Is Kay doing a census or a survey?
   Explain your answer.

> Explain your answer means write down why you decided it is a census (or a survey).

3 Justin wants to investigate the attitude to further education among the students in his class.
He decides he needs to interview all the students in his class.
He has four weeks to complete the task.
Give two reasons why this is unmanageable.

4 Faith has planned a coursework task.
As part of the task she wants to time how long it takes to get to her school from fifty different places.
Write down two reasons why this could be unmanageable.

5 Ravi wants to investigate the statement
'People prefer to shop at the supermarket outside the town rather than in the town centre.'
Ravi decides he will get information by questioning people in the supermarket and in the town centre.
Is this a survey or a census?
Explain your answer.

Summary of key points

Before you start a statistical investigation you need to decide:
- whether the question you are trying to answer can be answered using statistical methods
- what information you need and whether you can get that information
- whether you can get all the possible information or only some of it
- if the task is manageable.

Most students who get GRADE E or above can:
- decide if a question can be answered using statistical methods,
- make a hypothesis.

Most students who get GRADE C can also:
- decide what primary and/or secondary data is needed.

Glossary

Census	information from all possible items being investigated
Data	factual information
Hypothesis	a statement that may or may not be true
Primary data	factual information collected in person
Sample	some, but not all, of the items being investigated
Secondary data	factual information provided by someone else
Survey	investigation based on a sample

2 Collecting data

This chapter will show you:
✓ the difference between qualitative and quantitative data
✓ the difference between discrete and continuous data
✓ how to design a data collection sheet
✓ how to choose a sample
✓ how to design a questionnaire

Before you start you need to know:
✓ common units for length, mass and time
✓ how to add and subtract whole numbers
✓ how to simplify a fraction

2.1 Types of data

There are two main types of data.

Qualitative data is data that can only be described in words.

The gender and colour of a group of cats are examples of qualitative data.

Quantitative data is data that can be described using number values.

Height and shoe size are examples of quantitative data.

Qualitative data is also called categorical data.

Exam practice 2A

1. Harry wants to collect this information on apple trees.
   In each case write down whether the data is qualitative or quantitative.
   a If the apples on a tree are eating or cooking apples.
   b The weight of apples harvested from each tree.
   c The number of apples harvested from each tree.

2. Mark wants to collect this information about television viewing habits.
   In each case write down the type of data.
   a The time spent watching each day.
   b The type of programmes watched.
   c The number of television sets in the house.

3. Data is collected about each of these.
   In each case write down whether the data is qualitative or quantitative.
   a The lengths of pencils.
   b The lowest temperatures reached each night.
   c The times taken to wait for a bus.
   d The shapes of table tops.

Choose from qualitative or quantitative.

2.2 Data collection sheets

Data collection sheets are used to record information.

Example 1

Max spun this spinner.
He recorded the results on this table.

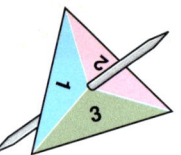

A **tally** mark records the score when the spinner is spun. Tally marks are easier to count when they are grouped in fives.

Score	Tally	Frequency
1												12
2														14
3											11
	Total	37

Add the tally marks in this row to find the number of times 2 is scored. This is called the **frequency**.

The completed table is called a **frequency table**.

a How many times did Max get a score of 2?
b How many times did Max spin the spinner?

Add together the frequencies to find out how many times Max spun the spinner.

a 14
b 37

Exam practice 2B

1 Angus asked some people to choose one of the colours Red, Blue or Yellow.
   He recorded their choices in this table.

Colour	Tally	Frequency
Red	||||	
Blue	|||| ||||	
Yellow	|||| ||	
	Total	

Count the tally marks next to Blue and put that number here.

a How many people chose blue?
b Copy the table and fill in the frequency column.
c Write down the number of people that Angus asked.

2 Vera used this table to record the GCSE grades of some students.

GCSE grades	Tally	Frequency
D	|||| ||||	
E	|||| |||| ||||	
F	|||| ||	
G	|||	
	Total	

a Write down the number of students who got grade D.
b Copy and complete the table.
c How many students' grades are there in the table?

3 Greg wanted to know how many CDs, DVDs and Video Tapes he sold one day.
He recorded the numbers on this tally chart.

	Tally	Frequency
CDs	ЖЖ ЖЖ ЖЖ IIII	
DVDs	ЖЖ ЖЖ III	
Video Tapes	ЖЖ ЖЖ ЖЖ II	
	Total	

a How many CDs did Greg sell?
b Copy the table and fill in the frequency column.
c Find how many more CDs than DVDs he sold.

4 Terry used this table to record the number of brothers and sisters of each person in a group.

Number of brothers and sisters	Tally	Frequency
0	ЖЖ III	
1	ЖЖ ЖЖ I	
2	ЖЖ IIII	
3	ЖЖ III	
4	II	
	Total	

a Copy and complete the table.
b How many people had no brothers or sisters?
c How many people did Terry ask?

2.3 Designing a data collection sheet

Before you start to collect data, you need to design a table on which you can record the information.

You will need three columns.

One for listing the items you are going to count, one for tally marks and one for the frequencies.

Example 2

Three coins are flipped.
Design a table to record the number of heads showing.

Each column needs a heading.

You can get 0, 1, 2 or 3 heads when you flip three coins. You need a row for each possibility.

Number of heads	Tally	Frequency
0		
1		
2		
3		
	Total	

Add a box for the total of the numbers in this column.

Exam practice 2C

1. A sample of people were asked to choose a colour from yellow (Y), green (G) or pink (P).
   a Design a table to record the information.
   b Use this list of choices to complete your table.
      Y G P Y Y P G G Y P P P
      G G Y G P G G Y Y P P Y
      P Y P P P Y P Y G Y G G
   c Which was the most popular colour?

   The first column will list the colours. Don't forget to add a column for the tally marks and the frequencies.

   Do not go through the list looking for all the Ys, then Gs etc. Work down the columns (or across the rows) marking a tally for each colour.

2. a Design a table to record the shoe sizes of a sample of 10-year-old children.
      (Use shoe sizes from 29 to 32.)
   b Use this list of shoe sizes to complete your table.
      32 31 32 31 29 32 30 30 31 30 31
      30 29 31 30 30 29 32 29 30 31 31
      29 30 31 31 30 29 30 32 31 30 29

   You do not know what the largest number of children is going to be. Add some blank rows to the table to cope with this.

3. Design a table to record the number of children in a sample of families.

4. The table shows the numbers of buses, cars and lorries that passed a bridge.

Vehicles passing bridge 9 a.m. to 10 a.m.	
	Frequency
Cars	150
Lorries	70
Buses	20

   a How many more cars than lorries passed the bridge?
   b Work out the number of vehicles that passed the bridge.

5 This table shows the results of an investigation into the number of days off work.

Days off for the week ending 03/10/05	
Number of days	Frequency
0	50
1	8
2	2
3	1
4	0
5	1

a How many people were investigated?
b How many people took more than one day off work?

> More than one means 2, 3, 4 or 5.

Mini coursework task
You need an ordinary six-sided dice.
Design a data collection sheet to record the results when the dice is rolled.
Now roll the dice 50 times and record the results.

2.4 Grouped data

Grouped data is used when there are too many different values to be listed separately, such as examination marks.

Example 3

The table shows a set of examination marks.

Marks	Tally	Frequency
0 – 10	ЖН	5
11 – 20	ЖН ΙΙ	7
21 – 30	ЖН ЖН ЖН Ι	16
31 – 40	ЖН ЖН ЖН ЖН ΙΙΙ	23
Total		51

> Remember the groups must not overlap.

> This row gives the number of marks between 21 and 30. Add the tally marks in this row.

> Add the tally marks in the other two rows. Then add all the frequencies.

a How many marks are between 21 and 30?
b How many marks are shown in the table?
c One mark of 24 was missed out.
   Which group does this mark go in?

    a 16
    b 51
    c 21 – 30

> 24 is between 21 and 30.

Exam practice 2D

1. This table was used to record the scores of teams in each round of a quiz.

Score	Tally	Frequency
0 – 10	|||| |||| |||| |||| ||	
11 – 20	|||| |||| |||| |||| |||| |||	
21 – 30	|||| |||| |||| |||| ||||	
	Total:	

   a. Copy and complete the table.
   b. Write down the number of scores recorded.
   c. How many times was more than 20 scored?

   More than 20 means 21 and higher.

2. This table gives the number of sentences in the paragraphs of a book.

Number of sentences	Tally	Frequency
1 – 5	|||| |||| |||| ||	
6 – 10	|||| ||||		
11 – 15	|||| |||	
16 – 20	||	
	Total:	

   a. Copy and complete the table.
   b. How many paragraphs had less than 6 sentences?
   c. How many paragraphs had more than 10 sentences?

   Less than 6 means 1, 2, 3, 4 or 5.

3. The marks in an examination are given in the table.

Mark	Tally	Frequency
0 – 10	|||| |||| |||| ||	
11 – 20	|||| |||| |||| |||| ||	
21 – 30	|||| |||| |||| |||| |||| |||	
31 – 40	|||| |||| ||||		
41 – 50	|||| |||| |||| ||||	
	Total:	

   a. Copy and complete the table.
   b. How many of the marks are more than 30?
   c. How many of the marks are from 0 to 20?
   d. How many marks are recorded in the table?
   e. Zoe asked how many marks are less than 25.
      Give a reason why Zoe cannot get this information from the table.

4   The frequency table shows the number of times a cash machine was used each day.

Number of withdrawals	Frequency
1 – 20	8
21 – 40	12
41 – 60	20
61 – 80	17
81 – 100	3

The first row tells you that there were 8 days when there were from 1 to 20 withdrawals.

a   On how many days were there more than 60 withdrawals?
b   Write down the total number of days.
c   Val said 'There were 30 days when there were fewer than 50 withdrawals.'
Explain why she cannot know this from the table.

5   A general knowledge quiz is marked out of 30.
These are the marks scored.

12 13 18 25 23 17 23 27 17 15 12 19 29 30
24   2   7   6 22 11   5 11 15 26 18 17   9 26

Design a table to record the marks of a sample of adults taking this quiz.

The lowest mark is 2 and the highest mark is 30.
So you can use the groups
0–10, 11–20, 21–30 .

6   This is a list of the number of letters in each word from a paragraph in a book.

6   4   6   3   7   4   6   4   1   3   5   3   4
4 10   5   6   4   3   6   7   8   4   5   3   1
9   5   6   3   7   1 12   1   1   9   4   1 15

a   Design a table to record this information.
b   Write down the number of words in the paragraph.

7   A cinema has 50 seats.
Design a table to record the number of seats sold for each performance.

2.5 Discrete and continuous data

There are two types of quantitative data.

Discrete data has only certain and exact values.

Shoe sizes are an example of discrete data. They have exact, separate values like 39, 40, $40\frac{1}{2}$. There is no shoe size between 40 and $40\frac{1}{2}$.

Continuous data has values anywhere in a range.

Heights are an example of continuous data. A normal adult's height can be anywhere between 1 m and 2.5 m, so a height can be any value in a range.

A height cannot be measured exactly.

Data such as lengths and times are continuous.

To collect data on the heights of men, first decide on a range that will cover all possible heights.
The heights of men are likely to be in the range 1 m to 2.5 m.
You can break this range into smaller sections.
These sections are called **class intervals**.

The class intervals must cover all possible heights between 1m and 2.5 m. This means that there must be no gaps.
You can break the range into intervals of width 0.5 m.
You need to be careful how you write these intervals.
If you write them as 1–1.5
                     1.5–2
                     2–2.5
you have included a height of 1.5 m (and 2 m) twice.

To avoid this you start the first class interval at 1 m then go up to, but do not include, 1.5 m. This class interval is written as $1 \leq h < 1.5$, where h metres stands for any height.

The next class interval can then start at 1.5 m and go up to, but not include 2 m. You write this as $1.5 \leq h < 2$.
This makes sure that there is no gap between the intervals and that there is no overlap.

The symbol $\leq$ means 'less than or equal to' and the symbol $<$ means 'less than'.

Example 4

Sam wants to collect the heights of some men.
a Design a table for Sam to record these heights.
b In which class interval would a height of 1.5 m be recorded?

a

Height, h metres	Tally	Frequency
$1 \leq h < 1.5$		
$1.5 \leq h < 2$		
$2 \leq h < 2.5$		

b $1.5 \leq h < 2$

Any height from 1 m up to but NOT including 1.5 m goes here.

This is where a height of 1.5 m goes.

These are the class intervals.

Exam practice 2E

1 This list gives the weights of some books. The weights are in grams.

   45   52   71   95   51   38   44   62   80   72
   81   39   48   60   66   75   36   63   92   108
   25 115   95   91   56   72   61   97 110   88

a Copy and complete this frequency table.

Weight, w g	Tally	Frequency
$20 \leq w < 50$		
$50 \leq w < 80$		
$80 \leq w < 110$		
$110 \leq w < 140$		

Do not go through the list looking for all the weights less than 50 g, etc. Work down the columns (or across the rows) making a tally mark for each weight in turn.

b How many books weighed less than 80 g?

2 The table shows the heights of some plants.

Height, h cm	Frequency
$15 \leq h < 18$	7
$18 \leq h < 21$	12
$21 \leq h < 24$	24
$24 \leq h < 27$	5
$27 \leq h < 30$	3

a How many plants were less than 21 cm high?
b How many plants were at least 24 cm high?
c One of the plants is 25 cm high.
  In which class interval is this height recorded?
d Find the number of plants whose heights are recorded in this table.

3 Jason wants to record the times for a 100 metre race.
The times are likely to be between 8 seconds and 20 seconds.
Design a table with four class intervals where these times can be recorded.

Do not forget to include a tally column and a frequency column. Remember to give the columns headings.

4 This table is used to record the weights of some grapefruit.

Weight, g grams	Tally	Frequency
$200 \leq g < 210$	|||| ||||	
$210 \leq g < 220$	|||| ||||		
$220 \leq g < 230$	|||| |||| ||||	
$230 \leq g < 240$	|||| ||||	

Two more grapefruit with weights 208 grams and 230 grams are included.
a Copy the table and add tally marks for the two extra grapefruit.
b Complete your copy of the table.
c How many grapefruit are there altogether?

5 The table shows the times that Lucy had to wait for a tram each morning.

Time, t minutes	Frequency
$0 \leqslant t < 5$	6
$5 \leqslant t < 10$	10
$10 \leqslant t < 15$	3
$15 \leqslant t < 20$	1

a One morning Lucy waited 8 minutes.
 Write down the class interval where this time is recorded.
b Write down the number of mornings on which Lucy had to wait 10 minutes or longer.
c Write down the number of mornings when Lucy had to wait less than 5 minutes.

6 This table shows the weights of some women.

Weight, k kg	Frequency
$40 \leqslant k < 60$	35
$60 \leqslant k < 80$	121
$80 \leqslant k < 100$	36
$100 \leqslant k < 120$	10

a How many women weigh between 60 and 80 kilograms?
b One of the women in this sample weighs 85 kg.
 Write down the class interval in which her weight is recorded.
c How many weights are recorded in the table?
d **i** How many of these women weigh under 100 kg?
    ii What proportion of these women weigh under 100 kg?

> Proportion means the same as fraction. This means that you need to put the number of women with weights under 100 kg over the total number of women, then simplify the fraction.

2.6 Collecting related data

A **two-way table** is used to collect two sets of related information. A two-way table has the values for one set of information across the top and the values for the other set down the side.

Example 5

Javid wants to collect information about house ownership among men and women.
The two sets of information he wants are

- Does a person own a house or not?
- Is the person male or female?

Design a data collection sheet for Javid.

	Owns a house	Does not own a house
Male		
Female		

A man who owns a house would be recorded here.

A two-way table can also be used to record grouped data.
This two-way table is designed to record the salaries and ages of some people.

This means £0 up to, but not including, £10 000

This means £50 000 or more.

	Salary					
Age, y years	£0 –	£10 000 –	£20 000 –	£30 000 –	£40 000 –	£50 000 –
$20 \leqslant y < 30$						
$30 \leqslant y < 40$						
$40 \leqslant y < 50$						
$50 \leqslant y < 60$						
$60 \leqslant y < 70$						

A person between 30 and 40 years old and earning between £20 000 and £30 000 a year is recorded here.

As you collect the information, you can add the tally marks. Then you can redraw the table and put in the totals.

Exam practice 2F

For questions 1–6 design a two-way table to record the information described.

1. Some men and women are asked whether or not they can swim.
2. Internet connections can be either direct dial or broadband. Some businesses and home users are asked which type of internet connection they have.
3. The number of bathrooms and the number of bedrooms in a sample of houses.
4. The gender (male or female) and the number of credit cards owned by a sample of people.
5. The ages of men and of women in full time work.
6. The weights and heights of children starting primary school. Start the heights at 90 cm and the weights at 20 kg.
7. The flowers on geraniums are either white, pink or red. Design a two-way table to record the colour of flowers and the heights of geranium plants three months after planting. Assume the heights start at 21 cm and stop at 60 cm.
8. Diran wants to test the hypothesis 'the number of television sets in a house is related to the number of rooms in the house.' Design a two-way table on which Diran can record the number of rooms and the number of televisions in a house.

You cannot legally be in full-time work until you are 16.

2.7 Sampling

When you want to collect data you need to decide if you can get all the possible information or only some of it.

> A **census** is information about all possible items being investigated.

> A **sample** is some, but not all, the possible items. A **survey** is an investigation that uses a sample.

Did you know that the government is the only organisation that can demand and get information from everyone? It does this once every ten years in a National Census.

A **representative** sample reflects all of the items being investigated. An **unrepresentative** sample does not reflect all of the items being investigated.

Any results from an unrepresentative sample will be **biased**.

Example 6

Julie reads that the council want to make the town centre a traffic-free zone between the hours of 8 a.m. and 10 p.m. She wants to investigate what support there is for this plan.

a Give reasons why Julie will have to use a sample.

b Julie chooses her sample by asking people in the town centre in the evening.
Give one reason why this is unrepresentative.

> **a** Julie will have to use a sample because she cannot get answers from everyone who goes to or lives in the town centre. This is because some people will refuse to give any information and some people will give incorrect information.
> She cannot be certain that she can ask everyone living in the town and even if she could it would take far too long.
>
> **b** Some groups of people, such as parents with young children, are unlikely to be included.

When you choose a sample, you must try to avoid bias by not leaving out any category.

 Exam practice 2G

1. A survey on voting intentions in a local election was conducted by telephoning people between the hours of 9 a.m. and 5 p.m. Give one reason why the sample may not be representative.

2. A survey into attitudes to a ban on cars in the city centre was conducted by asking the opinions of people coming out of the car park.
Give one reason why the sample will not be representative.

Think of one group of people that cannot be reached by telephone at those times. Write down a short sentence giving this group as your reason. For example 'People who ... will not be part of the sample.'

3 A survey into the number of passengers in a car was conducted outside a school.
Give a reason why this sample may not be representative of all cars on the roads in the town.

4 Gina measures the heights of the trees growing in her street.
Give a reason why heights of these trees are unlikely to be representative of all trees in the town.

5 A survey at a railway station found that two-thirds of the people questioned did not own a car.
This survey was used to claim that two-thirds of the people living in the town did not own a car.
Give a reason why this claim is likely to be biased.

6 Kate read that adults spend more than £30 a week on eating out. This was based on a survey carried out in a restaurant.
Explain why this result is likely to be biased.

7 A survey about car ownership was carried out at an out-of-town shopping mall.
Give a reason why the findings are likely to be unrepresentative.

8 Sunifa is investigating the connection between obesity and ill health. She decided to carry out a survey of people attending an outpatients clinic at the hospital.
Explain why her sample may not be representative.

9 A survey to find the times that adults spent on exercise each week was carried out at a gym.
Give a reason why this sample may not be representative.

10 A local council conducted a survey to find opinions on services that could be reduced to save money. The survey was carried out at an out-of-town supermarket and the local library.
Write down one group of people whose views would not be likely to be included.

2.8 Questionnaires

A **questionnaire** is a form that needs answers written on it.

Questionnaires are useful when you want to get opinions. They make sure that everyone is asked the same questions. But you need to be careful what questions you ask.

Ask questions that will be answered, and answered truthfully.
Add a box for the answer - this is called the **response**.

You may need more than one response. It is usually best to give several answers so that people can tick one of them.

| How old are you? ☐ years | ← This is a personal question; some people will refuse to answer this, some people will lie. Avoid questions like this. |

If you want this information, ask people to tick one of a range of ages. →

How old are you?
☐ Under 18 years
☐ 18 to 30 years
☐ Over 30 years

- Ask open ended questions that do not expect a certain answer.

| Don't you agree that cars should be banned from the town centre? Yes ☐   No ☐ | ← This is a leading question; it is worded to expect the answer yes. It is not suitable. |

This is a better question. It does not lead people to any particular answer. It also gives the option of not having to answer Yes or No. →

Should cars be banned from the town centre?
Yes ☐   Don't know ☐   No ☐

- Ask questions where the answers expected are obvious.

| Why are you in the town centre? ☐ | ← This question is not clear. It isn't obvious what information is wanted. |

This is clearer. It gives the information that is wanted. →

Why are you in the town centre? You can tick more than one box.
☐ Work   ☐ Shopping
☐ Meet friends   ☐ Eating out
☐ Entertainment ☐ Live here
☐ Personal business

- Write the responses so their meaning is exact.

| How long do you expect to be in the town centre?
☐ A short time
☐ An average amount of time
☐ A long time | ← The responses are not clear. They mean different things to different people. |

The responses asked for here are clear and obvious. →

How long do you expect to be in the town centre?
☐ Less than 2 hours
☐ Between 2 and 6 hours
☐ More than 6 hours

When you design a questionnaire, you cannot be sure that the questions are free of problems. Always try them out on a few people so that you can find problems and correct them before you start to collect the information.

Chapter 2 | Collecting data | 21

Exam practice 2H

  1 A questionnaire contained this question.

> What is your shoe size?

Write down one reason why this question is likely to give problems.

  2 A questionnaire contained this question.

> Don't you agree that children should always walk to school?

Explain why this question is not suitable for a questionnaire.

3 A questionnaire contained this question.

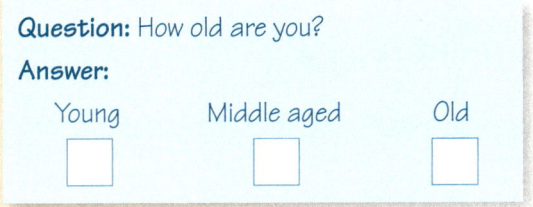

  a Explain why the question is likely to give problems.
b Give one reason why the headings on the boxes are not suitable.

4 A questionnaire contained this question.

> How did you do in your maths homework yesterday?

This question can have more than one meaning.
Write down two possible meanings.

5 Rachael wants to carry out a survey into what people eat at lunch time.
She designed this question to include in her questionnaire.

> How much do you eat at lunch time?

  a Explain why this question is not clear.
b Design a better question for Rachael to ask.
Include three responses.

Class discussion

A survey was carried out on attitudes to making the Town Centre a pedestrian only area.
The questionnaire used asked these questions:
  Do cars cause pollution?
  Is crossing the roads dangerous because of the traffic?
  Should the Town Centre be made pedestrian only?
Explain why you think that the three questions taken together are unsuitable.

Summary of key points

- You cannot always get all the information you need.
- When you can use only part of the possible information you must try to make sure that it is representative.
- Data can be qualitative or quantitative.
- Quantitative data can be discrete or continuous.
- Information can be grouped.
- Data collection sheets can be designed to record information.
- A two-way table can be used to record two related sets of information.
- Questionnaires are used to collect several pieces of information.

Most students who get GRADE E or above can:
- design and use collection sheets for grouped data.

Most students who get GRADE C can also:
- design a question with responses for a questionnaire,
- give reasons why a method of choosing a sample is unrepresentative.

Glossary

Bias	not chosen by chance
Census	information about all possible items
Class interval	range for continuous data
Continuous	able to have any value within a range
Discrete	exact and separate values
Frequency	the number of times that a value (or group of values) occurs
Frequency table	a table listing the possible values, or groups of values, and their frequencies
Qualitative	can only be described using words
Quantitative	can be described using numbers
Representative	reflects all of the items being investigated
Sample	a selection of items
Survey	an investigation using a sample
Tally	a mark used for counting
The symbols $<$ and $\leq$	'less than' and 'less than or equal to'
Unrepresentative	not reflecting all of the items being investigated

3 Representing data 1

This chapter will show you:
- ✓ how to draw and interpret a pictogram
- ✓ how to draw and interpret a bar chart for discrete data
- ✓ how to draw and interpret a frequency polygon for discrete data
- ✓ how to draw and interpret a frequency polygon for grouped data

Before you start you need to know:
- ✓ how to add and subtract whole numbers
- ✓ how to scale axes and plot points
- ✓ the meaning of fractions

3.1 Pictograms

A **pictogram** (or pictograph) is an eye-catching way of presenting **data** by using pictures.

A pictogram is easier to follow than looking at lots of numbers.

Example 1

This pictogram shows the number of hours of sunshine one day in July.

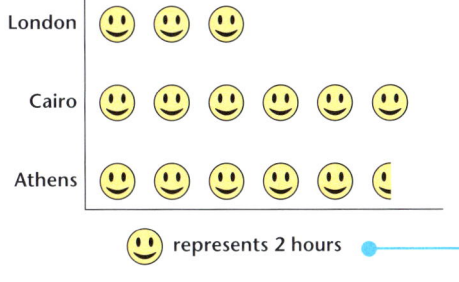

Number of hours of sunshine one day in July

☺ represents 2 hours

This is the key. It tells you what each symbol represents.

a Which city had the most sunshine?
b How much more sunshine was there in Athens than in London?

a Cairo.

There are 6 complete suns opposite Cairo. This is more than both of the others.

b 5 hours.

Each sun represents 2 hours of sunshine. There are $5\frac{1}{2}$ suns for Athens representing 11 hours of sunshine and 3 for London representing 6 hours of sunshine.

Exam practice 3A

1 Look at this pictogram.

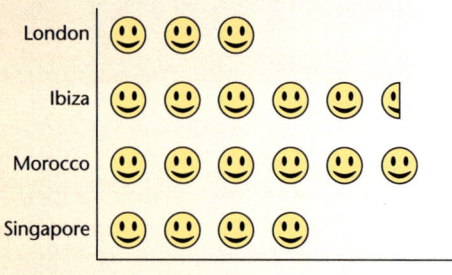

a How many hours of sunshine were there in London?
b Which place had the most sunshine?
c Which place had the least sunshine?
d How much more sunshine did Ibiza have than Singapore?

> Half a face represents 1 hour.

2 Look at this pictogram.

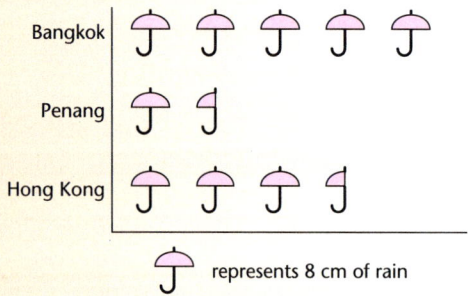

a Write down the name of the wettest place.
b How much rain did they have in Hong Kong?
c Write down the amount of rain they had in Penang.

> How much rain does half an umbrella represent?

3 This pictogram shows the road deaths at an accident black spot over four years.

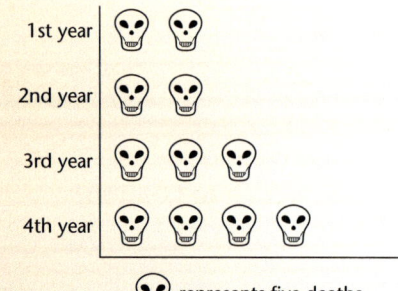

a Write down the number of deaths in the first year.
b How many more deaths were there in the third year than in the first year?
c Which year had the greatest number of road deaths?
d What message is the poster trying to tell you?

4 Study this pictogram.

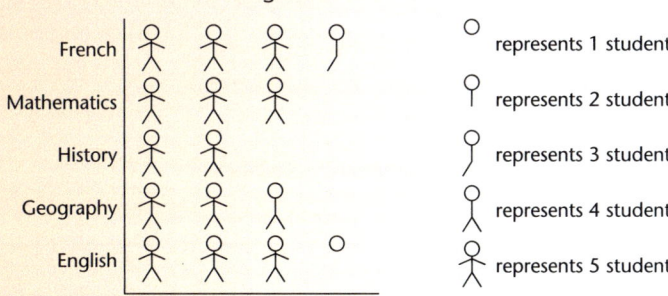

a Write down the most popular subject.
b Write down the least popular subject.
c How many students chose English?
d How many students chose French?

Look at the key.

5 This table shows the number of letters delivered by a postman in Westside Gardens.

Day	Number of letters delivered
Monday	16
Tuesday	18
Wednesday	24
Thursday	14
Friday	20

a How many letters were delivered in total from Monday to Friday?
b Draw a pictogram to show the data in the table.
   Use ✉ to represent 4 letters
   and ◺ to represent 2 letters.

For Monday you need to find how many 4s there are in 16. Now draw 1 full letter to represent each group of 4 letters, and so on for the other days.

Don't forget to add a key and a title.

6 Sally asked her friends what their favourite hobbies were. Her results are given in this tally chart.

Hobby	Tally
Sport	|||| |||| ||||	
Dancing	||||	
Pop music	|||| |||
Other	|||| |||| ||

a How many friends chose sport as one of their hobbies?
b How many friends did Sally ask?
c Draw a pictogram to show Sally's results.
   Use the symbol 🙂 to represent 4 people.

3.2 Bar charts for ungrouped data

Bar charts are used to illustrate frequency tables.
Bar charts come in many forms. The bars may touch each other, they may overlap or they may be lines. Sometimes the bars are horizontal. The bars must always be the same width.

A bar chart contains the same information as a **frequency table**.

Example 2

This bar chart shows the number of brothers and sisters for each student in a group.
How many students have 1 brother or sister?

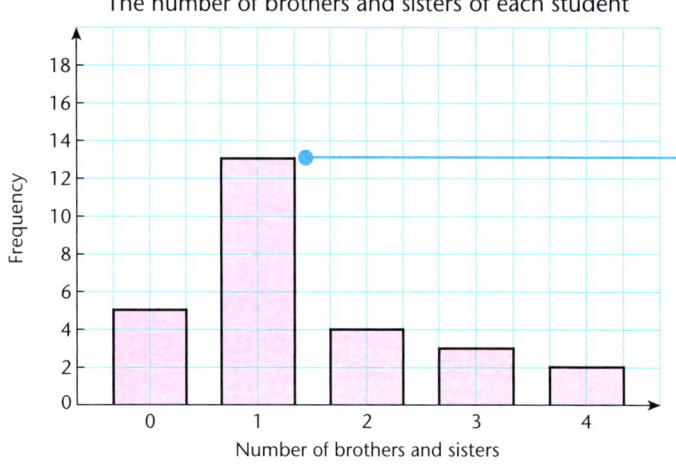

> This bar chart has a title which describes the information given. Each axis also has a **label** which shows what each set of numbers stand for.

> This bar comes up to 13 on the **frequency** scale.
> It is standing on 1 brother or sister. This means that there are 13 students who have one brother or sister.

13 students have 1 brother or sister.

Exam practice 3B

1 This bar chart shows the results from a maths test.

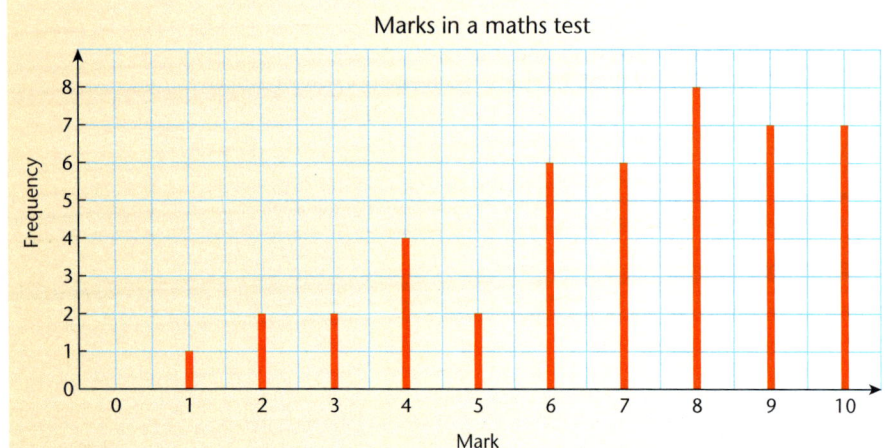

> Read the title and the labels on the axes carefully to make sure that you understand what information is shown.

a   Write down how many students had a mark of 8.
b   i   What was the lowest mark given?
    ii How many students got it?
c   Write down the most common mark.
d   How many students had a mark of 8 or more?
e   How many students took the test?

> Find 8 on the 'mark' line. Now go to the top of the line and go across to the frequency.
> Find the tallest line.
> '8 or more' means 8, 9 and 10.

2   In a survey, students were asked to choose their favourite subject. The results are recorded in this bar chart.

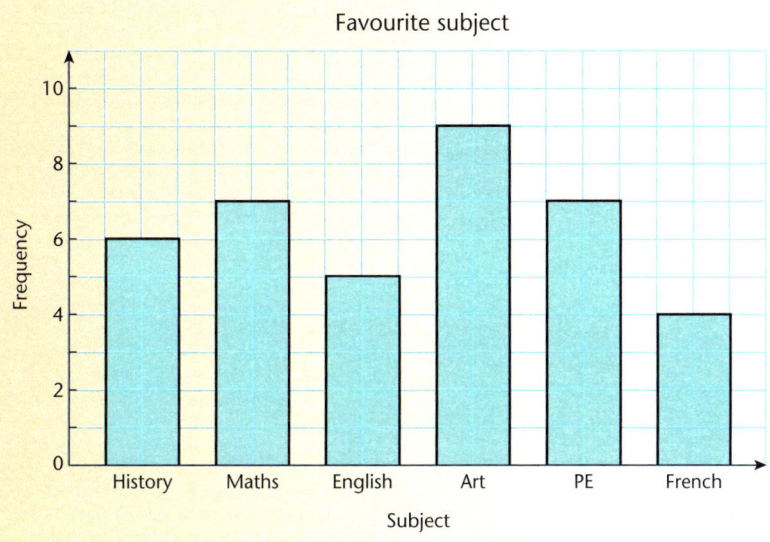

a   Write down how many students chose English as their favourite subject.
b   What was the most popular subject?
c   What was the least popular subject?
d   How many students took part in the survey?

3   This bar chart shows the pets owned by the students in a class.
    a   What is the most popular pet?
    b   Write down the number of dogs that were counted.
    c   What is the total number of pets owned by the members of the class?

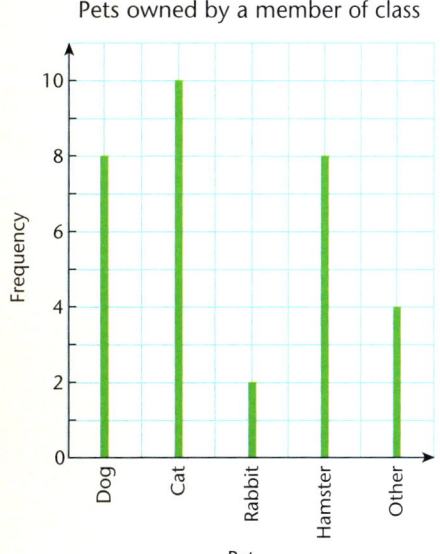

4 This bar chart shows the population in five towns.

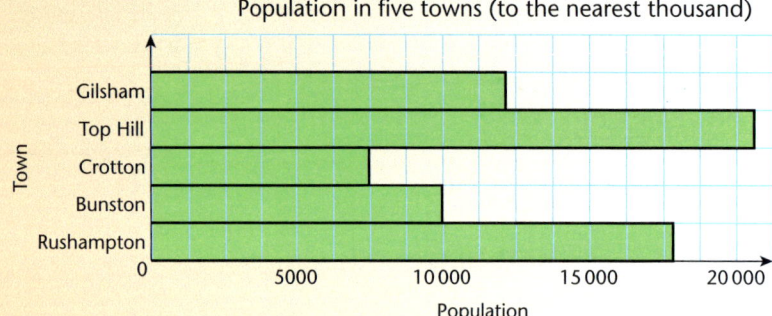

a Write down the town with the largest population.
b Write down the population of Bunston.
c i Which town has the smallest population?
   ii Write down the population of this town.

5 This bar chart shows the profits made by Airland Ltd.

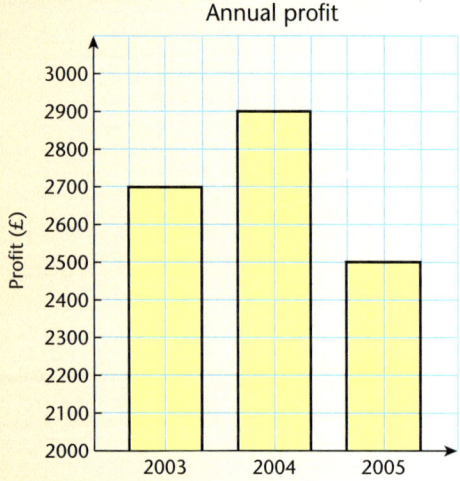

a Write down the profit in 2005.
b Write down how much more the profit was in 2004 than in 2003.

> First find the profits in 2004 and 2003. Now find their difference.

6 This bar chart shows the points scored by four football clubs in a league.

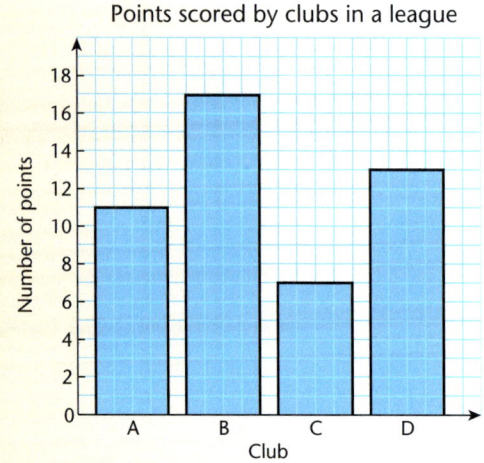

a Write down the club that has scored the lowest number of points.
b Write down the number of points scored by the most successful club.
c How many more points did club B score than club D?

3.3 Drawing bar charts

You can draw a bar chart from a frequency table.

Exam practice 3C

1. Joe asked his friends their favourite colour.
   Their answers are shown in this table.

Favourite colour	Frequency
Red	7
Blue	3
Green	5
Yellow	1

   Draw a bar chart to show Joe's results.

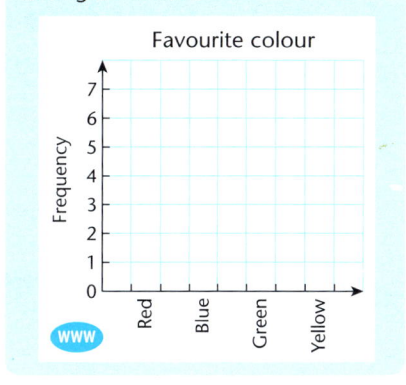

Use a grid like this.

2. Ian did a survey on children's opinions about the quality of school dinners.
   His results are shown in this frequency table.

Opinion	Very good	Good	Satisfactory	Poor	Very poor
Frequency	2	12	20	10	8

   a Write down the number of children in the survey.
   b Draw a bar chart to show the information.

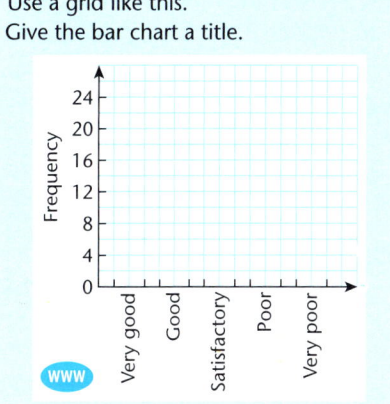

Use a grid like this.
Give the bar chart a title.

3. Terry asked his friends what their favourite hobby was.
   Their choices are shown in the table.

Hobby	Football	Computers	Pop Music	Other
Frequency	20	6	8	11

   a Write down the number of friends Terry asked.
   b Which hobby is the most popular?
   c Draw a bar chart to show the information.

When you draw a bar chart:
- give it a title
- label the axes
- make each bar the same width.

4 The students in a geography group got the following grades in an exam.

Grade	A	B	C	D	E
Frequency	4	8	11	5	2

a How many students sat the exam?
b Draw a bar chart to show this data.

5 Peter did a survey of the types of vehicles passing the school gate one lunch hour.
His results are shown in this table.

Type of vehicle	Bicycle	Motorbike	Car	Lorry
Frequency	4	10	25	16

a Calculate the number of vehicles that passed the school gate altogether.
b Which type of vehicle was the most common?
c Draw a bar chart to show the information.

Mini coursework task

Kerry said 'Fewer babies are born in January, February and March than in September, October and November.'
a Write down the information you need to test Kerry's hypothesis.
b Collect the information from at least 30 people.
c Show your information on a bar chart.
d Do you think Kerry is right?
e Give a reason for your answer.

3.4 Frequency polygons for ungrouped data

A **frequency polygon** uses points joined with straight lines to show information.

Example 3

The number of puppies per litter born at a kennel in a year was recorded.
This **frequency table** shows the results.

Number of puppies	0	1	2	3	4	5	6
Frequency	2	5	8	12	3	2	1

Draw a frequency polygon to show these results.

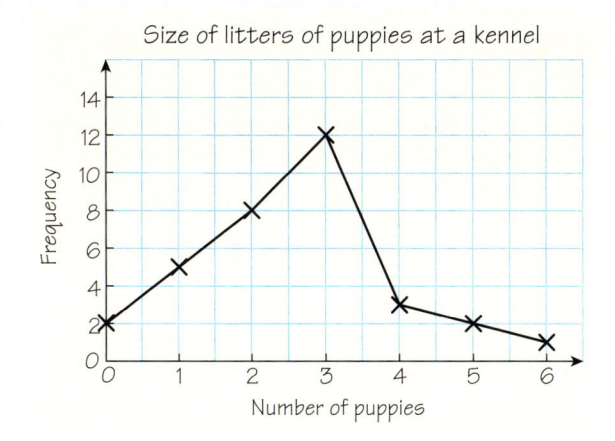

Size of litters of puppies at a kennel

(Frequency polygon plotted with points at (0,2), (1,5), (2,8), (3,12), (4,3), (5,2), (6,1); x-axis: Number of puppies; y-axis: Frequency)

Treat each number of puppies and its frequency as a pair of coordinates.
Plot these coordinates on a grid.
Finally join the points in order with straight lines.

Exam practice 3D

1 This frequency polygon shows the number of letters delivered to each house in a street.

Number of letters delivered to each house in a street

(Points plotted at (1,18), (2,26), (3,15), (4,10), (5,8), (6,6))

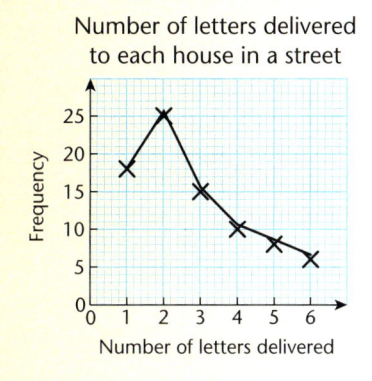

Go up from 4 on the horizontal axis. Now go across to the vertical axis. Read off the value.

   a Write down the number of houses in the street receiving just one letter.
   b Write down the number of houses in the street receiving exactly 4 letters.
   c Calculate the number of houses in the street receiving more than 4 letters.

2 The students in a class were asked how many bedrooms they had at home.
The results are shown in the table.

Number of bedrooms	1	2	3	4	5
Frequency	1	5	8	4	2

Draw a frequency polygon for this data.

Use a grid like this.
The first two points are plotted for you.
Don't forget to give a title.

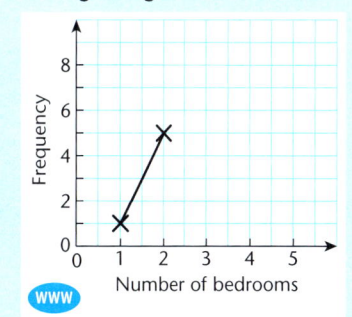

3 This table shows the number of goals scored by each of 32 teams in football matches one weekend.

Number of goals scored	Frequency
0	5
1	9
2	10
3	5
4	2
5	1

Draw a frequency polygon for this data.

Use a grid like this and give a title.

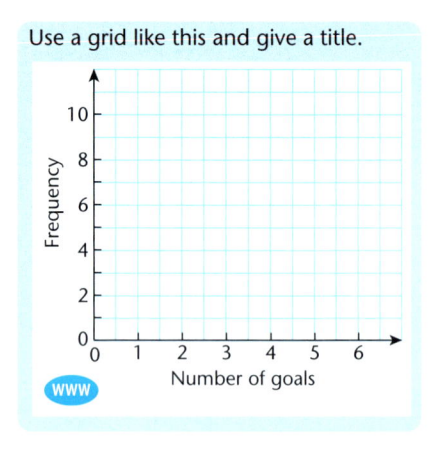

4 This table shows the number of GCSE subjects passed at grade C or better by some students.

Number of subjects at grade C or better	5	6	7	8	9	10
Number of students (frequency)	14	18	21	12	7	5

Draw a frequency polygon for this data.

Use a grid like this.

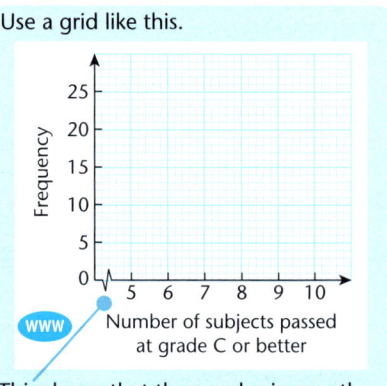

This shows that the numbering on the horizontal axis does not start at 0.

5 A sample of girls were asked their shoe size. The results are recorded in this table.

Shoe size	3	$3\frac{1}{2}$	4	$4\frac{1}{2}$	5
Frequency	2	5	10	8	4

a Write down the number of girls in the sample.
b Draw a frequency polygon for this data.

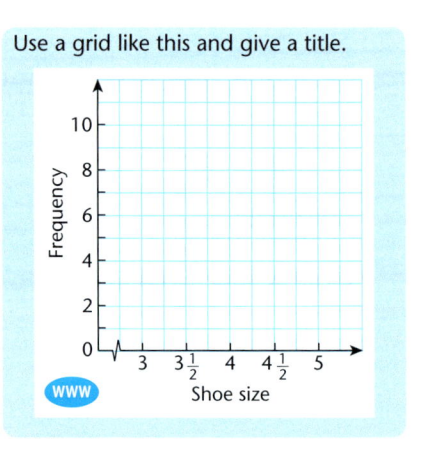

Use a grid like this and give a title.

6 The members of a Youth Club were asked 'How many holidays abroad have you been on in the last 5 years?'. Their answers are recorded in this table.

Number of times abroad on holiday	0	1	2	3	4	5
Number of families	12	18	8	4	2	1

a Write down the number of Youth Club members answering the question.

b Draw a frequency polygon to show this data.

3.5 Frequency polygons for grouped data

When you are using grouped data you sometimes need to know the value in the middle of a group (or class). This is called the **mid-interval value**.

When drawing a **frequency polygon** for grouped data you use the mid-interval value for each group.

The **mid-interval value** for a group is found by adding the end values of the group then dividing by 2.

Example 4

This **grouped frequency table** shows the numbers of letters in the words of a paragraph from a newspaper.

Draw a frequency polygon for this data.

Number of letters in a word	Frequency	Mid-interval values
1–3	15	2
4–6	12	5
7–9	6	8
10–12	2	11

Before you can draw a frequency polygon for this table, you need to find the value in the middle of each group. Add a column to the table for these values.

2 is half-way between 1 and 3.

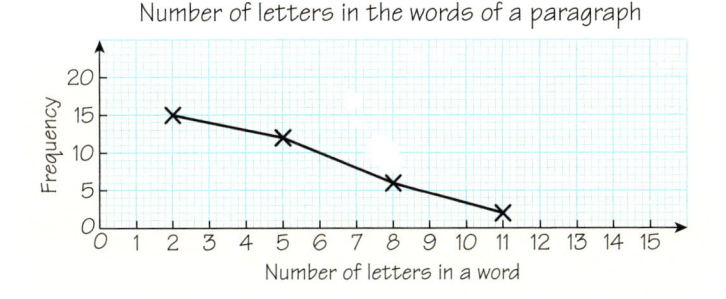

Treat the mid-interval value and the frequency as coordinates to plot the points on the grid. Join the points with straight lines.

Exam practice 3E

1 This table records the number of passengers on the buses that passed a survey point one day.

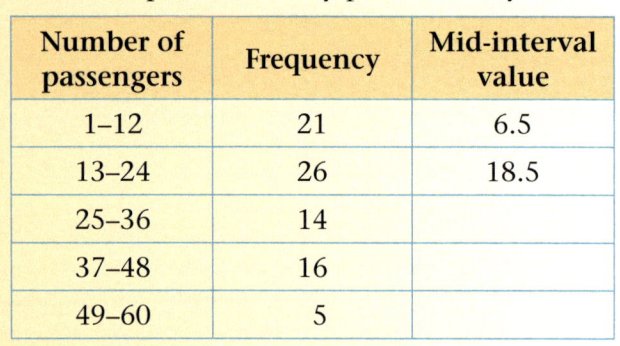

Number of passengers	Frequency	Mid-interval value
1–12	21	6.5
13–24	26	18.5
25–36	14	
37–48	16	
49–60	5	

a Copy and complete the table.
b Calculate the number of buses that passed the survey point.
c Draw a frequency polygon to show this data.

> The mid-interval value does not have to be a whole number of passengers. 18.5 is halfway between 13 and 24 so it is the mid-interval value.

> Use a grid like this. The first point is plotted for you.
> Number of passengers on buses
> (Frequency vs Number of passengers, point plotted at 10, 20)

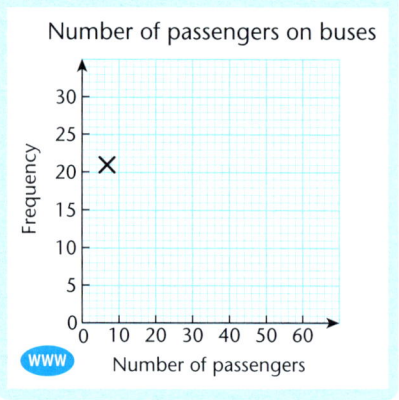

2 This table shows the number of competitors in a singing competition.

Number of competitors	Frequency	Mid-interval value
20–25	3	22.5
26–30	2	
31–35	12	
36–40	9	
41–45	5	

a Copy and complete the table.
b Calculate the number of times the competition has taken place.
c Draw a frequency polygon to show this data.

> Use a grid like this. The first point is plotted for you.
> Number of competitors in a singing competition
> (Frequency vs Number of competitors, point plotted at 22.5, 3)

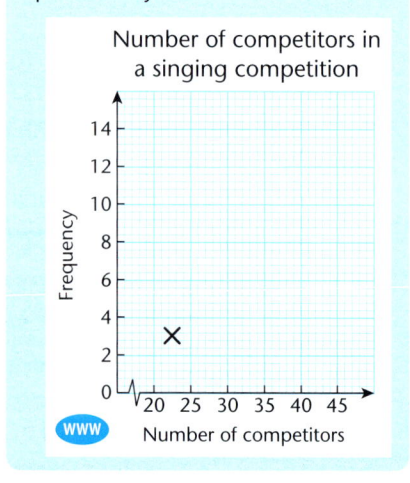

3 This frequency table shows the times taken by a sample of students to travel home one evening.

Time, t minutes	Frequency	Mid-interval value
$0 \leqslant t < 10$	3	5
$10 \leqslant t < 20$	10	15
$20 \leqslant t < 30$	5	
$30 \leqslant t < 40$	4	
$40 \leqslant t < 50$	2	
$50 \leqslant t < 60$	1	

a Copy and complete the table.

> This is continuous data. To find the mid-interval value, add the values of the ends of the class, then divide by 2.

b Copy the diagram and then use the values in your table to draw a frequency polygon.

Times taken by a group of students to travel home one evening

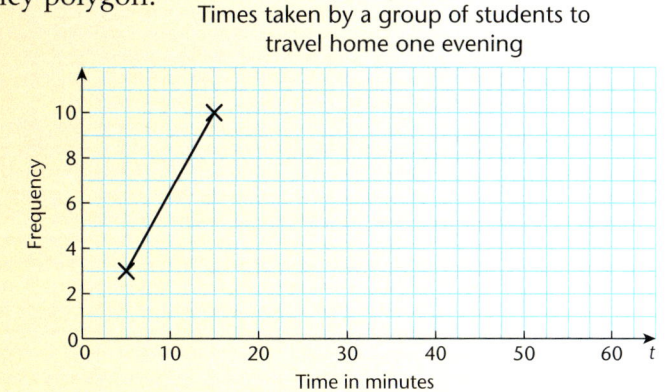

4 Kim recorded the lengths of 50 pea pods in this table.

Length, *l* cm	Number of pods	Mid-interval value
5 ≤ *l* < 7	8	
7 ≤ *l* < 9	14	
9 ≤ *l* < 11	19	
11 ≤ *l* < 13	9	

Use a grid like this.

Lengths of 50 pea pods

a Copy and complete the table.
b Use this information to draw a frequency polygon.

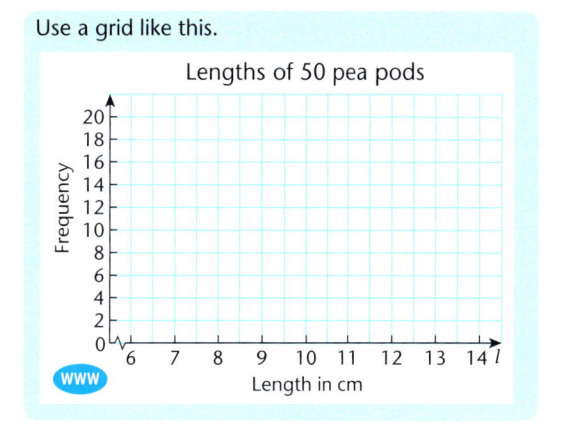

5 The number of playing members in 100 amateur soccer clubs is given in the table.

Number of players	Frequency (number of clubs)	Mid-interval value
10–20	8	15
21–31	32	
32–42	44	
43–53	16	

a Copy and complete the table.
b Draw a frequency polygon to show this data.

6 This frequency table shows the heights of a batch of tomato seedlings.

Height, *h* cm	0 ≤ *h* < 1	1 ≤ *h* < 2	2 ≤ *h* < 3	3 ≤ *h* < 4	4 ≤ *h* < 5
Mid-interval value					
Frequency	5	10	25	4	1

a Copy the table and complete the middle row.
b Draw a frequency polygon to show this data.

7 This frequency polygon shows the amounts of money spent in a butcher's shop by the customers one Saturday.

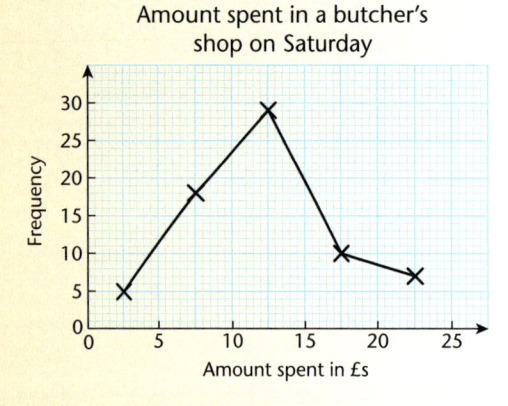

Amount spent in a butcher's shop on Saturday

a Calculate the number of customers on Saturday.

This table shows the amounts spent by customers on Wednesday.

Amount spent, A pounds	Number of customers
$0 \leq A < 5$	8
$5 \leq A < 10$	11
$10 \leq A < 15$	15
$15 \leq A < 20$	8
$20 \leq A < 25$	4

b Calculate the number of customers on Wednesday.
c Copy the frequency diagram above and use your copy to draw a frequency polygon for the amounts spent by customers on Wednesday.

Do not forget to add a column for the mid-interval values

8 This table shows the times taken by a group of students to complete a task.

Time (t minutes)	Number of students
$10 \leq t < 20$	5
$20 \leq t < 30$	25
$30 \leq t < 40$	20
$40 \leq t < 50$	10
$50 \leq t < 60$	7
$60 \leq t < 70$	3

Draw a frequency polygon for these times.

Summary of key points

- A pictogram uses simple drawings and is an easy way of comparing the sizes of different groups.
- The information in a frequency table can be shown in a bar chart or a frequency polygon.
- The heights of the bars give the frequencies.
- A frequency polygon is drawn by plotting points on a pair of axes to represent the frequencies of a set of data. The points are then joined in order.
- For a grouped frequency polygon the points are plotted at the mid-interval values.

Most students who get Grade E or above can:
- get information from bar charts and frequency polygons and draw them when scales are given.

Most students who get grade C can also:
- draw bar charts and frequency polygons when the scales are not given.

Glossary

Bar chart	shows bars of the same width whose heights give the frequencies
Data	factual information
Frequency	the number of times something happens
Frequency table	shows the number of times that each distinct value (or category) occurs
Frequency polygon	the shape obtained by joining the points in order that represent the frequencies of items or groups of items
Grouped frequency table	shows the frequencies of groups of values and the data can be discrete or continuous
Key	tells you what each symbol represents
Label	the meaning of the numbers on an axis
Mid-interval value	the middle value of a group
Pictogram	a way of presenting data by using pictures

4 Representing data 2

This chapter will show you:
- ✓ how to draw and interpret a pie chart
- ✓ how to draw and interpret a stem-and-leaf diagram
- ✓ what a time-series is
- ✓ how to get information from a time-series graph
- ✓ the meaning of an index number

Before you start you need to know:
- ✓ how angles are measured
- ✓ how to use a protractor
- ✓ that angles at a point add up to 360°
- ✓ the meaning of fractions and percentages
- ✓ how to read values from a graph
- ✓ how to plot points and draw a graph
- ✓ how to find a fraction of a quantity

4.1 Pie charts

A **pie chart** is a circle divided into slices.
It shows the proportion (share) that each group of **data** is of the whole.

Example 1

This pie chart shows how water was used in one household.

Water usage in a household

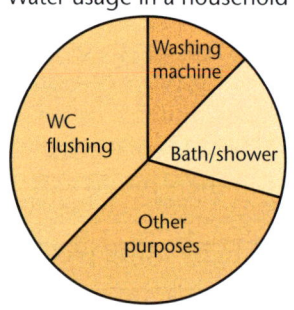

a Write down the purpose for which water is used least.
b Write down an estimate for the fraction used for baths or showers.
c Write down an estimate for the fraction that is used for 'Other purposes'.
d Write down one use of water that is likely to be included in 'Other purposes'.

a The washing machine. ← This is the smallest slice.
b $\frac{1}{6}$ ← The slice for 'Bath/shower' is about $\frac{1}{6}$ of the circle.
c $\frac{1}{3}$
d Washing the dishes. ← The slice for 'Other purposes' is about $\frac{1}{3}$ of the circle

Chapter 4 Representing data 2

Exam practice 4A

1 Andy paid a decorator £750.
This pie chart shows the breakdown of the bill.

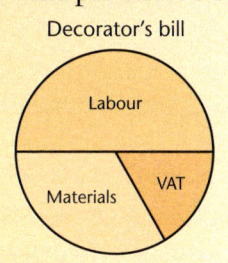

Decorator's bill (Labour, Materials, VAT)

a Write down the fraction of the bill that was for labour.
b Write down the cost of the labour.

Use your answer to part a to find the fraction of £750.

2 This pie chart shows the proportion of the votes that three candidates got in an election. Bennett got 1200 votes.

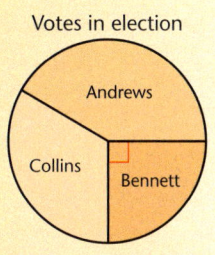

Votes in election (Andrews, Collins, Bennett)

a Roger said that Bennett got one quarter of the votes.
Is Roger correct?
Explain your answer.
b Calculate the number of votes altogether.

3 The pie chart shows how fuel is used in the average home.

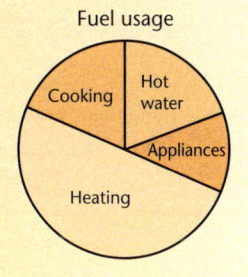

Fuel usage (Cooking, Hot water, Appliances, Heating)

a Write down the purpose for which most fuel is used.
b Write down the fraction of fuel used for heating.
c Which one uses more fuel: appliances or hot water?

Which is the largest slice?

What fraction is the slice of a circle?

4 100 students were asked if they read a daily newspaper.
The results of the survey are shown in the pie chart.

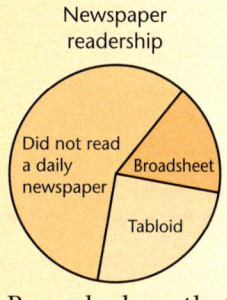

Newspaper readership (Did not read a daily newspaper, Broadsheet, Tabloid)

a Estimate the fraction of the students surveyed who read a tabloid.
b Estimate the number of students surveyed who read a tabloid.

5 Records show that 100 people have died on the roads of Westshire.
This pie chart shows those deaths, by category.

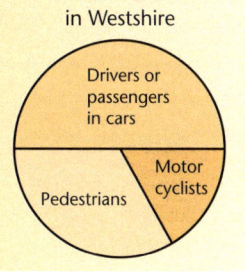

Road deaths in Westshire (Drivers or passengers in cars, Motor cyclists, Pedestrians)

a How many of the deaths were drivers or passengers in cars?
b Estimate the fraction who were pedestrians.

6 This pie chart shows the age distribution of the population of a town.
The population of the town is 10 000.

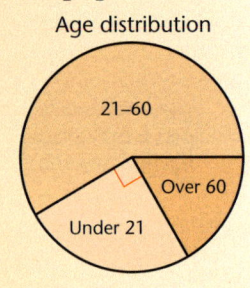

Age distribution

a Write down the fraction of the population under 21.
b Estimate the number of people under 21.
c Jerry said that there were more than 5000 people in the town in the 21–60 age group. Is Jerry correct?
Give a reason for your answer.

7 This pie chart shows the number of bedrooms in each of the homes of a group of students.

Bedrooms in students' homes

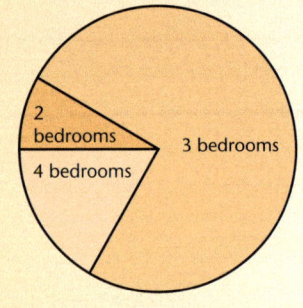

$\frac{3}{4}$ have 3 bedrooms at home.

$\frac{1}{6}$ live in a home with 4 bedrooms.

12 students have 4 bedrooms.

a How many students are there altogether?
b How many students are there living in a home with 3 bedrooms?
c How many are living in a home with 2 bedrooms?

> The second and third facts tell you how many students make $\frac{1}{6}$ of the whole. You can use this information to find the total number of students.

8 Sabina paid £1440 for her car to be repaired.
This pie chart shows how the cost was divided.

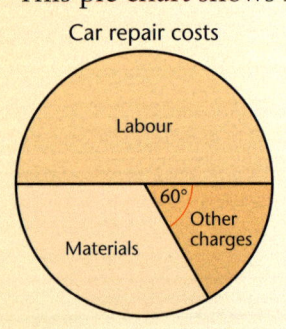

Car repair costs

a Work out the fraction of the bill that was for other charges.
b Work out the amount of the other charges.

9 This pie chart shows the passengers on a coach.
There were 15 children.

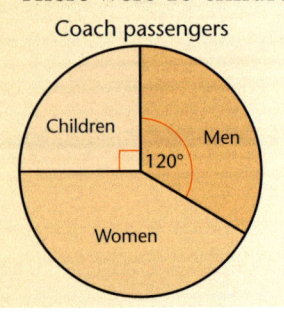

Coach passengers

a Vejay said that one-third of the passengers were children.
Is Vejay correct? Give a reason for your answer.
b Keri said that there were the same number of men as women.
Is Keri correct? Give a reason for your answer.

> Find the angle representing the women.

4.2 Drawing pie charts

A pie chart can be drawn from a frequency table.
The frequencies are used to work out the angles for each slice.

Example 2

This frequency table shows the foods bought in the school canteen by 36 pupils.

Food	Frequency
Salad	9
Pizza	12
Burger	15
Total	36

Represent this data on a pie chart.

Food	Frequency	Angle at centre
Salad	9	9 × 10° = 90°
Pizza	12	12 × 10° = 120°
Burger	15	15 × 10° = 150°
Total	36	Total: 360°

This acts as a check on your working

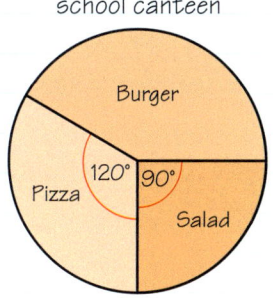

You need to work out the angle at the centre for each slice.
There are 36 pupils, so 1 pupil gets an angle of 360° ÷ 36 = 10°.
This means that 9 pupils need an angle of 9 × 10° = 90°, and so on.
Add a column to the table to put these values in.

Now you can draw the pie chart.

Draw a circle and one radius. Make your circle big enough to use a protractor. Use a radius of 5 cm or more.

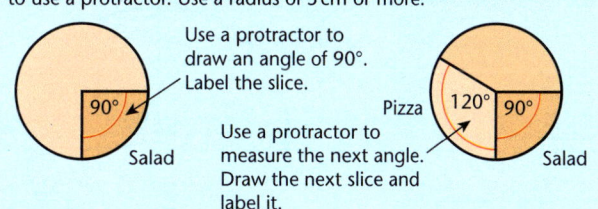

Use a protractor to draw an angle of 90°. Label the slice.

Use a protractor to measure the next angle. Draw the next slice and label it.

Continue until you get to the last slice.
This angle should be 150°. You can measure this to check that the drawing is accurate.
Do not forget to give the chart a heading.

Foods bought in the school canteen

Exam practice 4B

1. There were 90 men, women and students at a parents' evening. The table shows the number of each.

	Number	Angle at centre
Men	30	30 × 4° = 120°
Women	45	
Students	15	
Total	90	

Work out the angles for each slice. The total is 90 so each person is represented by $\frac{360°}{90} = 4°$.

Copy and complete the table and pie chart to show this data.

People at parents' evening

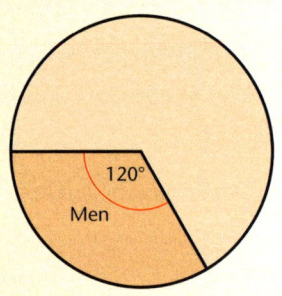

120° Men

Draw a circle with radius at least 5 cm. Then you will find it easier to use a protractor to measure the angles.

2 A box contains 60 coloured balloons. The table shows the numbers of each colour.

Colour	Number of balloons	Angle
Red	16	
Yellow	24	
Green	9	
Blue	11	
Total	60	

The angle for each balloon is $360° \div 60 = 6°$. You can use this to work out the angle for each slice. Use the empty column to record the angles.

Copy and complete the table and pie chart to show this information.

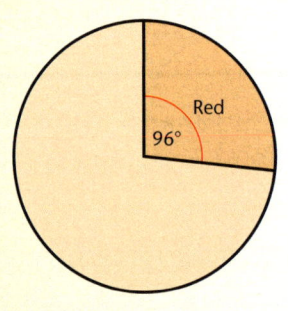

Red 96°

Remember to give a title.

3 Andy sells second-hand executive cars.
He recorded the numbers he sold last month.

Make	Frequency	Angle
BMW	15	
Mercedes	10	
Jaguar	5	
Audi	6	
Total		

Draw and label a pie chart to represent this information.

First find the total of the frequencies. Use this value to find the angle for each make of car.

Use a copy of the table to help you.

4 The table shows the ownership of shares in a family business.

Ownership	Number of shares (thousands)
John Price	14
Carol Price	9
Tim Brown	7
Total	

Draw and label a pie chart to represent this information.

Use a copy of the table to help you.

5 Sam did a survey of the shops in an arcade.
The number of each type is shown in the table.

Type of unit	Number
Clothes shops	19
Charity shops	10
Other	11

Draw and label a pie chart to represent this information.

6 Jake collects books.
The table shows how many of each type he has.

Type	Number of books
Fiction	170
Non-fiction	104
Reference	86

Draw and label a pie chart to represent this information.

ICT task
The weight of materials used in building a shed are:
wood 46.18 kg, glass 27.13 kg, roofing felt 12.27 kg, concrete 112.5 kg.
Enter this information into a spreadsheet.
Then use the spreadsheet to draw a pie chart.

4.3 Stem-and-leaf diagrams

A **stem-and-leaf diagram** (sometimes called a stem plot) is a way of grouping data without losing the detail of individual values.

Getting information from a stem-and-leaf diagram

This stem-and-leaf diagram shows the number of pages in a sample of books.

Number of pages   1 | 41 means 141

```
1 | 20 34 41 92
2 |  9 10 25 36 71 77 86
3 | 10 24 63
```

These numbers form the stem. They are like the groups in a frequency table.

These numbers are the leaves.

This is the key. It tells you that the 1 in the stem represents 100. The 'leaf' is added to give the value. So the 2 in the stem and the 'leaf' 9 represents the number 209.

Example 3

Use the stem-and-leaf diagram above to
a write down the number of books in the sample
b give the number of books that have more than 300 pages.

a 14

Count the number of 'leaves' to the right of the vertical line. There are 4 in the first row, 7 in the second and 3 in the third.

b 3

The last line shows all books with more than 300 pages. There are 3 entries.

Exam practice 4C

1 The weights of the packages to be delivered by a courier are given in this stem-and-leaf diagram.

   Weight
   ```
   0 | 93 95 98
   1 |  8 22 24 25 36 73 83
   2 | 14 44 52 88 99
   ```
   1 | 22 means 122 g

   a Find the number of packages the courier has to deliver.
   b Write down the weight of the lightest package.
   c Write down the number of packages weighing more than 200 g.

2 Cars were tested to see how long they took to reach 100 mph from a standing start.
   This stem-and-leaf diagram shows the results.

   Time in seconds
   ```
   1 | 2 4 4 7 9
   2 | 3 4 4 4 5 6 9 9
   3 | 0 1 1 4 6 6 8
   4 | 2 2 4 5 7 7
   ```
   2 | 3 means 23 seconds

   a Work out the number of cars tested.
   b Write down the slowest time.
   c Write down the fastest time.
   d Find the number of cars that took more than 30 seconds.

3 The times taken by the competitors in a race were recorded.
   They are shown in this stem-and-leaf diagram.

   Time to complete the race
   3 | 21 23 25 37 45 51   3 | 21 means 3 minutes 21 seconds
   4 | 3 4 4 12 15 34 42 53
   5 | 1 9 14 16

   a Write down the number of competitors who finished.
   b Write down the time taken by the person who was last.
   c How many times were less than $3\frac{1}{2}$ minutes?
   d Find the difference in the time taken by the person who was
      first and the one who was last.

   First you need to find the time taken by the slowest person and the time taken by the fastest person.

4 Ken recorded the number of cars in the station car park each
   morning when he went to work.
   This stem-and leaf diagram shows his records.

   Number of cars
   2 | 3 4 4 7 8   2 | 3 means 23
   3 | 2 3 6 6 8 9
   4 | 1 4 7 9

   a Write down the number of working days for which cars were
      counted.
   b How many days were there more than 30 cars in the car park?
   c Write down the number of days that there were fewer than 30
      cars in the car park.

4.4 Completing and drawing a stem-and-leaf diagram

Example 4

This list gives the number of cars in a car park at noon
on twenty consecutive Saturdays.

   104 99 107 102 115 102 108   98 110 106
   108 95   94 118   95 105 114 102 113   97

Draw a stem-and-leaf diagram to represent this data.

Number of cars in car park
 9 | 9 8 5 4 5 7
10 | 4 7 2 2 8 6 8 5 2
11 | 5 0 8 4 3

Number of cars in car park
 9 | 4 5 5 7 8 9   11 | 4 means 114
10 | 2 2 2 4 5 6 7 8 8
11 | 0 3 4 5 8

Decide on the groups to use for the stem. The numbers are all between 90 and 120, so we will use tens for the stem and units for the leaves. So 10 | 4 represents 104.

*Start working across the first row marking each value in the correct place.
Do not try to put them in order at this stage.
Check that you have 20 values.*

*Redraw the diagram with the numbers in order of size. Give a key and a heading.
Check again that you have 20 values.*

Exam practice 4D

1. A maths test was marked out of 40.
   This stem-and-leaf diagram shows the marks scored by students in the test.

   Marks

   ```
   1 | 4 4 5
   2 | 0 4 5 6 7 7 7
   3 | 0 0 1 2 3 3 4 4 4 4 4 5 5 8 9 9
   ```
   1|4 means 14

   a Calculate the number of marks shown in the diagram.
   b Write down the lowest mark.
   c Two other students got marks of 36 and 29.

   Copy the diagram and add these two marks in the correct place.

2. Meena timed her journey to school on seventeen days.
   These times are shown in this stem-and-leaf diagram.

   Time in minutes

   ```
   1 | 2 4 5 6 8 8 9        2|5 means 25 minutes
   2 | 0 0 1 1 5 7 9
   3 | 0 2 5
   ```

   a The next three days her times were 17 minutes, 19 minutes and 27 minutes.
      i Copy the diagram and add these three values to the stem-and-leaf diagram.
      ii Rewrite your stem-and-leaf diagram so that all the values are in order.

   Use your new diagram for these questions.
   b Write down the number of times the journey took
      i   more than 20 minutes
      ii less than 25 minutes
      iii longer than half an hour.

3. A school library bought some new books. This is a list of their prices.

   £4.50 £6.20 £5.40 £4.90 £5.70 £4.39
   £6.45 £5.95 £4.75 £5.80

   a How many new books were bought?
   b The first four prices in the list are shown in this stem-and-leaf diagram.

   Price of books

   ```
   4 | 50 90           5|40 means £5.40
   5 | 40
   6 | 20
   ```

   Enter the prices one at a time. Do this in order. First £4.50, then £6.20, then £5.40 and so on.

   Copy and complete the diagram to show all the prices.
   c Rewrite your stem-and-leaf diagram as an ordered stem-and-leaf diagram.

4 These are the recorded playing times, in minutes, of some CDs.

61 37 50 50 59 72 41 47 68 59 59 69 42
59 66 60 61 65 50 55 52 61 45 74 68 39

a How many CDs were recorded?
b Copy and complete this stem-and-leaf diagram to show these times.
The first time in the list has been entered.

Number of minutes

```
3 |
4 |                    6 | 1 means 61 minutes
5 |
6 | 1
7 |
```

c Rewrite the stem-and-leaf diagram so that the times are in order.
d How many of these CDs have playing times of less than 55 minutes?

5 The amounts spent by some students on lunch were:

£2.10, 75p, 89p, £1.56, £2.50, £1.90, £2.84, £2.70, £2.50, £2.55, £2.35 and £1.86

a How many students were there?
b Copy and complete this stem-and-leaf diagram.

The first amount has been entered for you.

Amount spent on lunch

```
0 |
1 |                    2 | 10 means £2.10
2 | 10
```

c Rewrite the stem-and-leaf diagram so that the amounts are in order.
d How many students spent more than £2 on lunch?

6 The number of mobile telephone calls received by a group of students one week were:

12, 16, 28, 25, 9, 19, 7, 6, 17, 4, 21, 18, 24, 13, 16

a How many students were there?
b Copy and complete this stem-and-leaf diagram. The first amount has been entered for you.

Number of calls received

```
0 |
1 | 2                  1 | 2 means 12
2 |
```

c Rewrite the stem-and-leaf diagram so that the numbers of calls are in order.
d How many students had more than 10 calls?

4.5 Reading time-series graphs

Data that changes over time is called a **time-series**.

Example 5

When Becky went into hospital her temperature was taken every hour and recorded on this **time-series graph**.

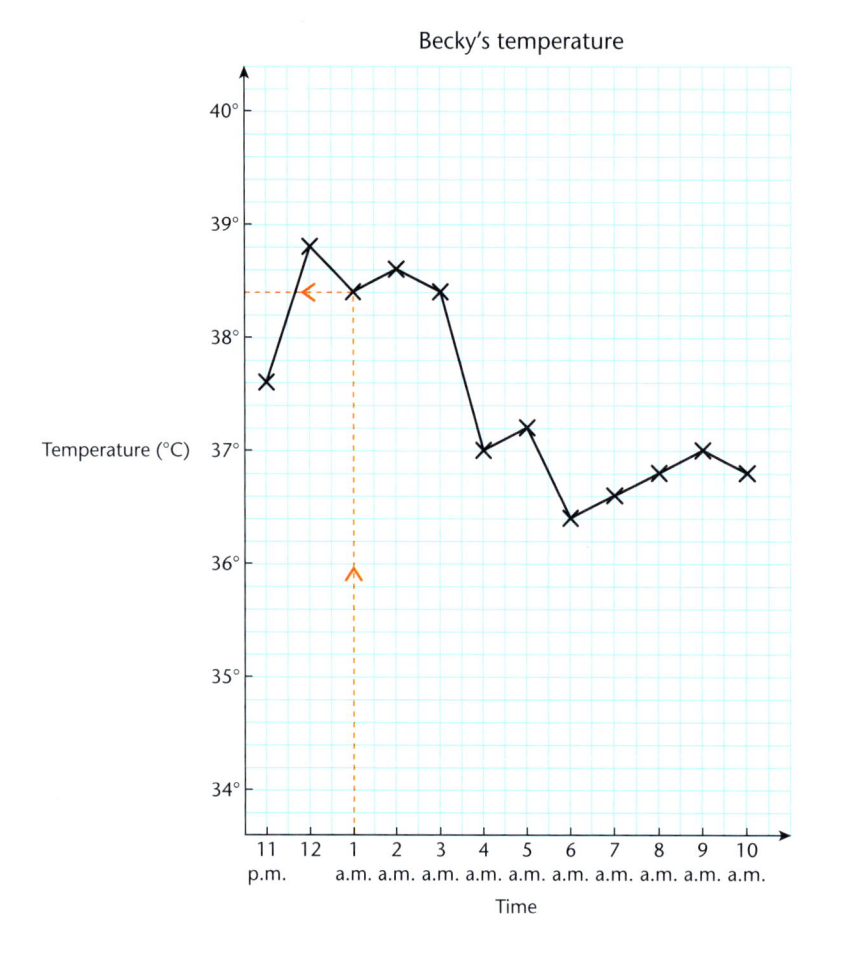

Becky's temperature

> A time-series graph allows you to see how the data is changing over time. You always record time on the horizontal axis.

a What was Becky's temperature at 1 a.m.?
b Can you use this time-series graph to find Becky's exact temperature at 3.30? Give a reason for your answer.

   a 38.4 °C
   b You cannot use the graph to find the exact temperature at 3.30 a.m. because it only records her temperature on each hour.

> You could use the graph to **estimate** Becky's temperature at 3.30 a.m. 37.6 °C is halfway between the recorded values at 3 a.m. and 4 a.m.

Exam practice 4E

1. Use the graph opposite to answer these questions.
   a i Write down Becky's highest recorded temperature.
      ii Write down when it occurred.
   b Write down her lowest recorded temperature.
   c At 8 a.m. her temperature was normal.
      Write down her normal temperature.
   d Work out how long she was in hospital before her temperature was recorded as normal.
   e Jo said that Becky's highest temperature while she was in hospital was 39 °C.
      Could Jo have been correct?
      Write down why you have answered 'yes' or 'no'.

2. 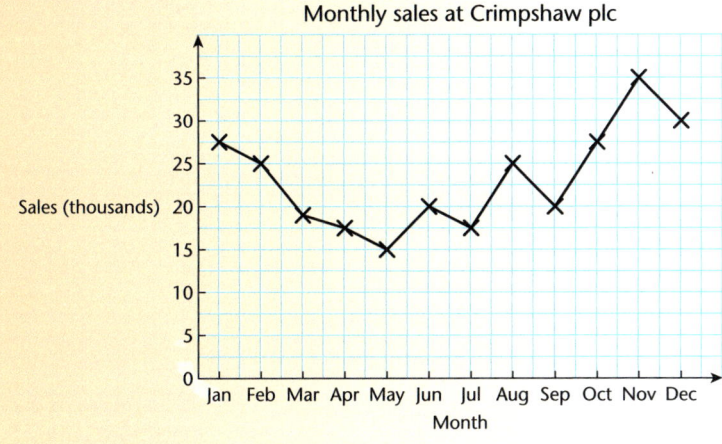

   Monthly sales at Crimpshaw plc

   (Line graph: Sales (thousands) vs Month. Values approximately — Jan 27, Feb 25, Mar 19, Apr 17, May 15, Jun 20, Jul 17, Aug 25, Sep 20, Oct 27, Nov 35, Dec 30.)

   The graph shows the total monthly sales in a hardware shop.
   a Write down the month when the sales were i greatest ii least.
   b Gemma said 'The sales improved around Christmas'.
      Is Gemma correct?
      Give a reason for your answer.

3. Tim was ill. His temperature was taken once every hour and recorded on this chart. 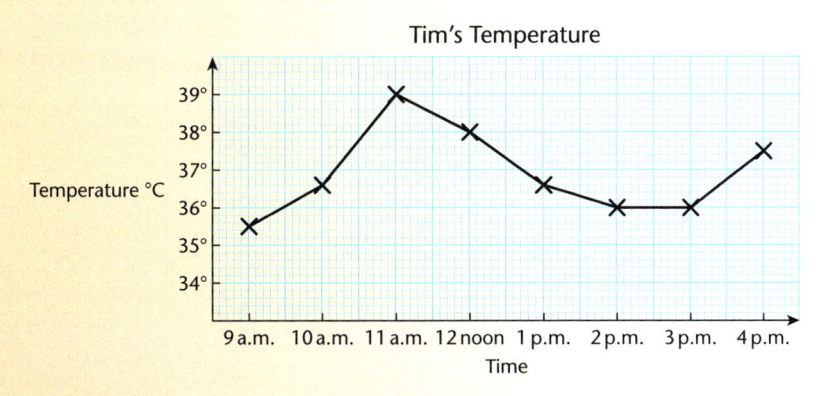

   Tim's Temperature

   (Line graph: Temperature °C vs Time. 9 a.m. 35°, 10 a.m. 36.5°, 11 a.m. 39°, 12 noon 38°, 1 p.m. 36.5°, 2 p.m. 36°, 3 p.m. 36°, 4 p.m. 36.5°.)

   a Write down Tim's temperature at i 11 a.m. ii 3 p.m.
   b Judy said 'Tim's temperature at 3.30 p.m. was 36.8°.'
      Was Judy correct? Give a reason for your answer.

4 The time-series graph shows the price of a share in DC Electronics at yearly intervals, since it was formed.

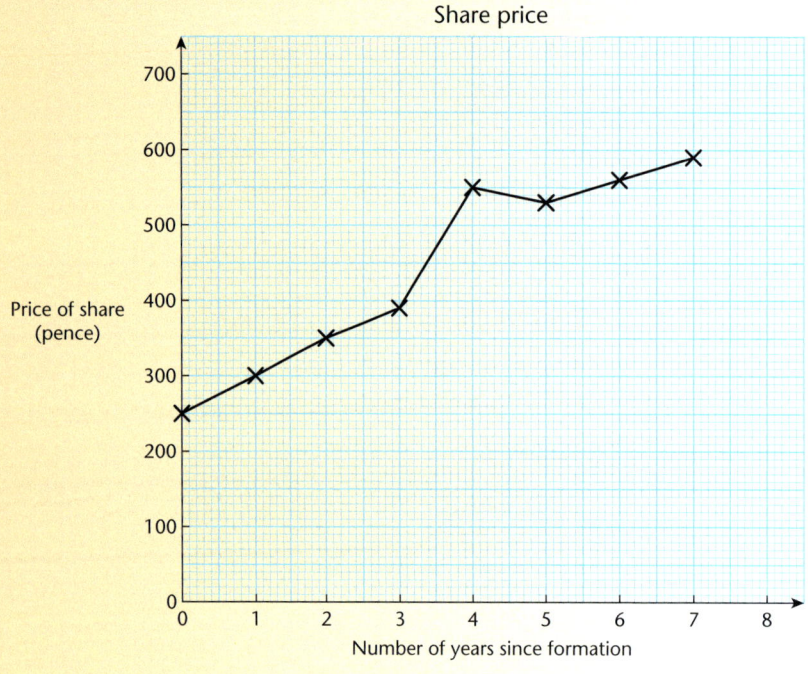

Share price

Price of share (pence) vs Number of years since formation

a Write down the starting price of the share.
b Copy and complete the following table.

Time after formation (years)	1	2	3	4	5	6	7
Share price (pence)	300	350					

c Between which years did the share price rise most?
d What trend do you notice in the price of the share?

Trend means 'Is the share price rising or falling or staying about the same?'

5 This time-series graph shows Fran's bank balance at the start of each month for 12 months.

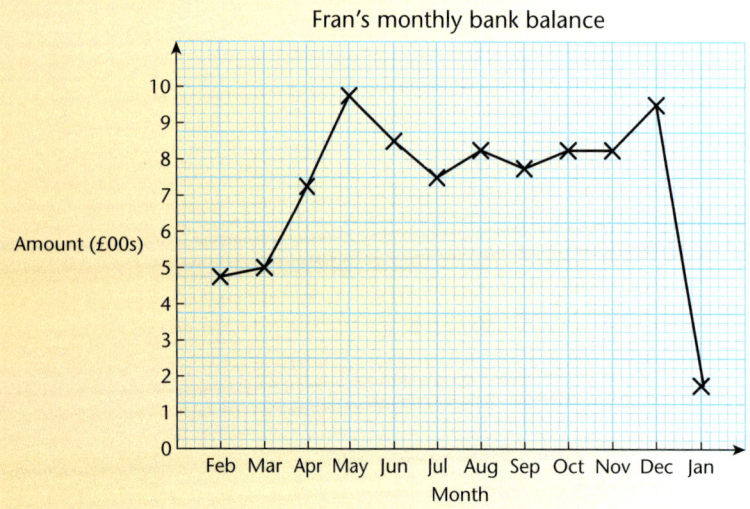

Fran's monthly bank balance

Amount (£00s) vs Month

a i Write down Fran's biggest recorded balance.
   ii Write down the month when this was.
b Write down the month in which her balance goes down most.

6 This time-series graph shows the number of students in a school getting grade F or higher in GCSE maths from 1996 to 2003.

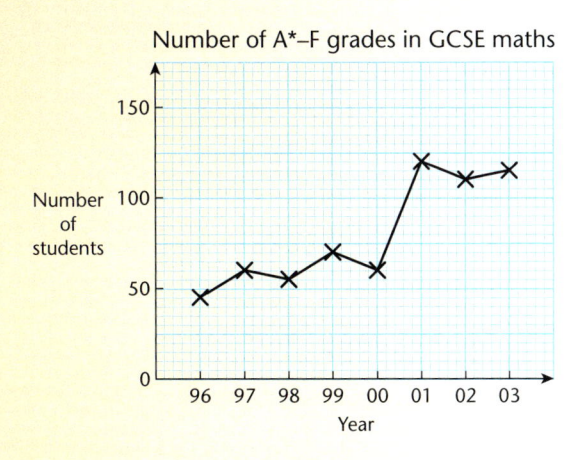

Number of A*–F grades in GCSE maths

a Write down the number of students who got grade F or higher in maths in 1997.
b Write down how many more students got grade F or higher in 2001 than in 1998.
c Mark said 'More than twice as many got grade F or higher in 2003 compared with 1996.'
Is Mark correct? Give a reason for your answer.

> You need to find the number who got grade F in 2001 and the number who got grade F in 1998.

7 This table shows the annual rainfall in Blackwood from 1995 to 2002.

Year	1995	1996	1997	1998	1999	2000	2001	2002
Rainfall (inches)	63	60	69	82	77	90	84	86

a Use a grid like this to plot these values on a graph.

Annual rainfall in Blackwood 1995–2002

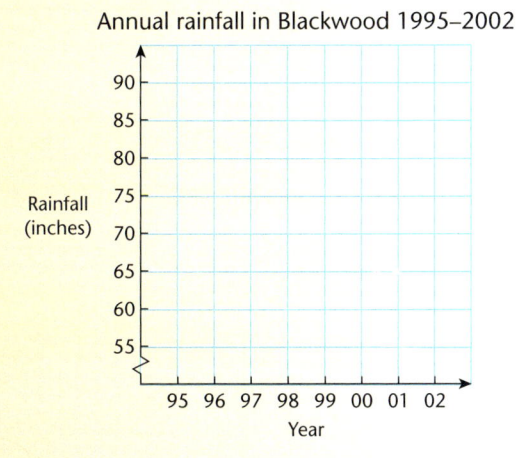

b Join the points with straight lines.
c Tony said that the annual rainfall in Blackwood is increasing.
Is Tony correct?
Give a reason for your answer.

8 This table shows the quarterly sales figures for a toyshop.

Year	2001				2002				2003			
Quarter	1	2	3	4	1	2	3	4	1	2	3	4
Sales (£thousands)	10	29	29	14	20	34	11	13	13	22	36	14

> The first quarter is for the months Jan to March; the second from April to June, and so on.

a Plot a time-series graph for this data.
b Fay said that sales are highest in the second quarter of the year.
   Is Fay correct?
   Give a reason for your answer.

9 This table shows the number of students at Durfield School.

Year	1994	1995	1996	1997	1998	1999	2000	2001	2002	2003
Number of students	1100	1150	1040	1050	1010	1000	960	980	940	900

a Plot a time-series graph for this data.
b Poppy said that the number of students in the school is falling.
   Is Poppy correct?
   Give a reason for your answer.

4.6 Index numbers

An **index number** is the percentage one quantity is of another but with the percentage sign left out.

Index numbers are usually used to show changes in prices.
The figure on which the percentage is calculated is called the **base**.

Example 6

The index for house prices in Carston now, compared with the year 2000 as base, is 152.

a Have house prices gone up or down in this time?
b By what percentage has the cost of an average house changed?

> The index has gone up from its base value (100) to 152.

a House prices have gone up.

b The cost of an average house has increased by 52%.

> An index of 152 compared with 100 means that it has increased by 52%

Exam practice 4F

1 The index for household fuel, compared with 1995 as base, is 146.
   a Has the price of fuel gone up or down?
   b By what percentage has the cost of household fuel changed?

2 Over a five year period the retail price index went up from 100 to 136.
   What percentage did the average retail price change over the period?

3 The index for the cost of clothing is 95 now compared with 100 last year.
   a Is the cost of clothing more or less now than it was last year?
   b By what percentage has it changed?
      Give a reason for your answer.

4 The cost of public transport today is 45% more than it was 8 years ago. The index 8 years ago was 100. What is the index for the cost of public transport now?

5 The cost of a DVD player is 20% lower this year than last year. What is the index for the cost of a DVD player today using last year as base?

6 The average cost of a computer has decreased from £500 to £250 during the last 10 years.
   a How much has the average cost of a computer gone down?
   b By what percentage has the average cost of a computer changed?
   c What is the price index today, taking the cost 10 years ago as the base?

Summary of key points

- Pie charts show each category as a fraction of the whole. The angle at the centre of a slice is the fraction of 360° that the size of the category is of the whole.
- Stem-and-leaf diagrams preserve individual values, unlike frequency tables, bar charts and pie charts.
- A time-series graph gives information about a quantity at specific times. It says nothing about the values in between.
- An index number can be used to compare the cost of the same thing at different times.

Most students who get GRADE E or above can:
- draw a pie chart
- understand a time-series chart.

Most students who get GRADE C can also:
- draw a stem-and-leaf diagram
- interpret index numbers.

Glossary

Data	factual information
Key	tells you what the stems and leaves represent
Pie chart	shows, as slices of a circle, what fraction of the whole each part is
Stem-and-leaf diagram	shows data organised into groups
Time-series	data that changes over time
Time-series graph	a graph that represents the data in a time-series
Index number	the percentage change in a quantity compared to a chosen base value

5 Range and averages

This chapter will show you:
- ✓ what the range of a set of numbers is and how to find it
- ✓ the meaning of mean, mode and median
- ✓ how to find the mean, mode and median of a set of numbers
- ✓ how to find the mean, mode and median from a frequency table
- ✓ how to find the mean and modal class for a grouped frequency distribution

Before you start you need to know:
- ✓ how to put a set of numbers in order
- ✓ how to add, subtract, multiply and divide whole numbers
- ✓ how to add and subtract decimal numbers
- ✓ how to divide a decimal by a whole number

5.1 Range

The **range** is the difference between the largest number and the smallest number.

Example 1

Tina got these marks in five tests:

 4, 6, 3, 8, 5

Find the range.

 $8 - 3 = 5$
 The range is 5 marks.

> The highest mark is 8 and the lowest mark is 3.

Exam practice 5A

1. Work out the range for each set of data.

   a Five students got these marks in a test:

    6, 8, 5, 7, 9

   b Val asked five friends how many pets they each had. Their answers were:

    2, 4, 1, 0, 1

> Find the difference between the highest value and the lowest value.

c The price of a can of coke in five different shops is:
       68p, 64p, 70p, 65p, 60p

  d Five people win the following amounts in a raffle:
       £10, £5, £6, £7 and £12

  e The ages, in years, of five children are:
       9, 10, 8, 10, 11

> You need to include units when writing the range.

2 Work out the range for each set of data.
  a The lengths of five leaves are:
       4.9 cm, 5.2 cm, 5.6 cm, 5.2 cm, 5.7 cm.

  b The number of people queuing at each checkout:
       4, 7, 9, 3, 5, 6, 4

  c The weights of some potatoes are:
       34 g, 45 g, 29 g, 21 g, 38 g, 42 g, 27 g

  d The heights of some plants are:
       2.1 m, 1.9 m, 2.4 m, 1.8 m, 1.9 m, 2.2 m

  e The number of pencils in each of nine pencil cases:
       3, 2, 5, 3, 6, 2, 8, 5, 4

> The range is longest length – shortest length.

> Write the numbers in order starting with the smallest. If you have your own list cross them off as you go.

5.2 Mode

The **mode** of a set of numbers is the number that occurs most often.

Example 2

These are some test marks.
   6, 4, 6, 8, 10, 6, 3, 8 and 4

Find the mode.

3, 4, 4, 6, 6, 6, 8, 8, 10
The mode is 6 marks.

> Put the numbers in order. Then you can see which is the most common.

Exam practice 5B

1 Find the mode for each set of data.
  a The ages of some children are:
       10, 12, 14, 12, 12, 8, 12

  b The number of sweets in each of ten packets.
       6, 9, 9, 7, 8, 6, 9, 9, 10, 8

> First write the numbers in order starting with the smallest. Now look for the number that appears most often.

c The lengths of some nails are:
   1.8 cm, 1.9 cm, 1.8 cm, 1.4 cm, 1.8 cm

d These are the number of pages in some books.
   58, 56, 59, 56, 63, 56, 59

You need to include units when writing the mode.

2 Find the mode for each set of data.
   a The weights of some pumpkins:
      5.9 kg, 4.9 kg, 5.6 kg, 5.9 kg, 5.8 kg, 4.5 kg, 3.7 kg
   b These are the lengths of some ribbons.
      26.4 cm, 26.7 cm, 26.4 cm, 26.5 cm, 26.4 cm.
   c The heights of 5 girls, correct to the nearest centimetre, are
      155, 148, 153, 154, 155
   d The weight, in tonnes, of some full skips are
      6.2, 5.3, 4.5, 7.0, 6.2, 5.5, 6.2

Remember to include units.

5.3 Median

The **median** of a set of numbers is the middle number when they have been placed in order.

When there are two middle numbers, the median is the sum of these two numbers divided by two.

Example 3

These nine students are arranged in order of their height.
Find their median height.

↑
Middle student

The median height is 155 cm.

The middle student is the fifth.

Example 4

The heights of 10 students arranged in order of height are:
146 cm, 148 cm, 151 cm, 151 cm, 156 cm, 157 cm, 159 cm, 162 cm, 162 cm, 165 cm.
Find their median height.

> (156 + 157) ÷ 2 = 156.5
> The median height = 156.5 cm

There are two middle numbers.

The median is the sum of these divided by 2.

Exam practice 5C

1. Find the median for each set of data.
   a. The numbers of people waiting in a surgery at 6 pm were
      26, 33, 39, 42, 64, 87, 90
   b. The number of people on a bus at each stop was
      13, 24, 19, 13, 6, 36, 17
   c. The number of calls made to '999' each hour was
      4, 18, 32, 16, 9, 7, 29
   d. The lengths, in centimetres, of a sample of screws are
      1.2, 3.4, 3.2, 6.5, 9.8, 0.4, 1.8
   e. Javid recorded how late his bus was each morning.
      These are his results.
      2 min, 2 min, 3 min, 5 min, 7 min, 11 min, 13 min

   Write the numbers in order starting with the smallest.

2. Find the median for each set of data.
   a. The numbers of items in six shopping baskets:
      5, 7, 11, 13, 17, 19
   b. These are the lengths of some wood off-cuts.
      34 cm, 46 cm, 88 cm, 92 cm, 104 cm, 116 cm, 118 cm, 144 cm

   The middle numbers are the 3rd and 4th.

3. The times taken by some apprentices to paint a door were
   34 min, 42 min, 16 min, 85 min, 97 min, 24 min, 18 min, 38 min.
   Find the median time.

4. These are the weights of some coins.
   1.92 g, 1.84 g, 1.89 g, 1.86 g, 1.96 g, 1.98 g, 1.73 g, 1.88 g.
   Find the median weight.

5. The number of children in each of 15 families is:
   1, 1, 1, 1, 2, 2, 2, 2, 2, 3, 3, 3, 4, 4, 5
   Find the median number of children.

6. A dice was rolled 10 times. These are the scores.
   2, 6, 4, 5, 3, 6, 6, 4, 3, 4
   What is the median score?

5.4 Mean

The **mean** or **arithmetic mean** is the most commonly used **average**.

To find the mean of a set of values find the sum of the values and divide by the number of values.

Example 5

Kay has 7 pens, Emily has 6 pens and Olivia has 11 pens.
Find the mean number of pens.

Total number of pens = 7 + 6 + 11
= 24
Mean number of pens = 24 ÷ 3
= 8

Mean number of pens
= total number of pens
÷ number of students

The mean is not always a whole number, or even a quantity that can exist.

Example 6

Ian has 2 dogs, Rajiv has 1 dog and Sarah has 1 dog.
Calculate the mean number of dogs.

The mean = $\frac{2+1+1}{3} = \frac{4}{3} = 1\frac{1}{3}$ dogs

If they could share the dogs equally, each of the three people would have $\frac{4}{3} = 1\frac{1}{3}$ dogs. This is clearly impossible. But $1\frac{1}{3}$ is the mean of the numbers 2, 1 and 1.

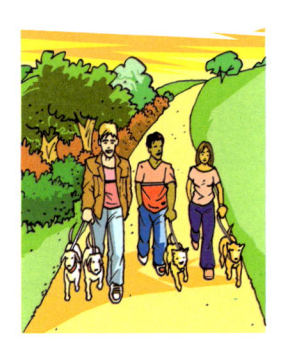

Exam practice 5D

1. Find the mean for each set of data.

    a Six pupils got these marks in a test:
       6, 7, 8, 4, 6, 5.

    Find the sum of these marks, then divide by the number of pupils.

    b In three different shops, the price of a can of lemonade is
       37p, 35p and 33p.

    Remember to include units.

2 Five people decided to share their money.
They put the following amount on a table:

£9, £5, £6, £8 and £12.

  a How much was on the table?

  b If each person had put in the same amount, how much would each have given?

  This means that you have to find the mean of the five amounts.

3 Find the mean for each set of data.

  a The ages, in years, of the children in a gym class are

  9, 9, 10, 8, 10, 11, 8, 12, 9, 10, 11, 11, 12.

  Be careful, there are a lot of numbers.

  b The number of calls to a call centre each minute were

  3, 4, 8, 4, 7, 1, 7, 6, 5, 5

  c The number of chocolates in some boxes are

  10, 15, 13, 10, 24, 18

4 Find the mean for each set of data.

  a The cost of some bottles of water are

  24p, 35p, 44p, 28p, 34p

  b The lengths of some nails are

  1.2 cm, 1.5 cm, 1.3 cm, 1.2 cm

  c The amount people spent one evening was

  £12.40, £16.50, £27.90, £3.50, £26.10

5 Karl measured the lengths of six leaves for a science project:

  4.9 cm, 5.2 cm, 5.6 cm, 5.2 cm, 5.7 cm and 5.2 cm.

  a Find the mean length of these six leaves.
  Karl measured four more leaves: 5.5 cm, 4.7 cm, 5.0 cm and 4.4 cm.

  b Find the mean length of these four leaves.

  c Find the mean length of all ten leaves.

5.5 Range, mode and median from frequency tables and diagrams

Frequency tables and bar charts showing ungrouped data give the information in order of size. The range and the mode are easy to find.

Pie charts showing qualitative data also show the mode clearly.

When the position of the middle item is not obvious, you can find it by adding 1 to the total number of items then dividing by 2:

The middle item is the $\frac{n+1}{2}$ th item where n is the total number of items.

Example 7

This table shows the number of words in each sentence on the first page of a book.

Number of words	Frequency
5	8
6	10
7	6
8	4
9	2
10	3
Total	33

Find **a** the range **b** the mode **c** the median.

a 10 − 5 = 5
Range = 5 words

> The range is the difference between the highest and lowest values. The highest number of words in a sentence is 10 and the lowest is 5.

b The mode is 6 words.

> The mode is the number of words with the highest frequency.

c $\frac{33+1}{2} = \frac{34}{2} = 17$, so the middle sentence is the 17th.
The median is 6 words.

> There are 33 sentences so the middle sentence is the 17th. Count down the frequencies until you find the 17th sentence. The first 8 sentences have 5 words. Adding on the next 10 gives 18 sentences. Therefore the 17th sentence is one of these.

Exam practice 5E

1 Write down the mode for each pie chart.
   a Fuel usage in homes 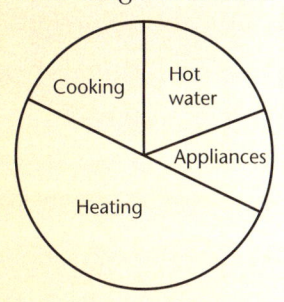
   b Computer usage

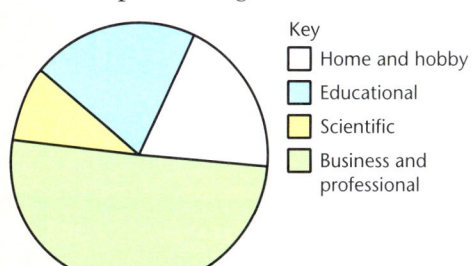

   Key
   ☐ Home and hobby
   ☐ Educational
   ☐ Scientific
   ☐ Business and professional

   > The mode is the label on the largest slice.

   c Eye colour

2 The table shows the marks in a test.

Mark	Frequency
1	1
2	3
3	6
4	5
5	2

Work out   **a** the range   **b** the mode   **c** the median.

> Write down your working when you find the median, even if you can do it in your head.

3 The table shows the shoe sizes of some children.

Shoe size	Frequency
33	15
34	10
35	13
36	8

Work out   **a** the range   **b** the mode   **c** the median.

4 Once every 10 minutes Nia counted the number of people waiting at a bus stop.
Her results are shown in this table.

Number of people at a bus stop	Frequency
0	3
1	7
2	5
3	2
4	2

Work out   **a** the range
b the mode
c the median number of people queuing.

5 Gary counted the number of customers eating in his restaurant each day. The table shows the results.

Monday	Tuesday	Wednesday	Thursday	Friday	Saturday	Sunday
8	14	12	18	25	30	12

a Work out the range in the number of customers.
b Which day is the modal day?

6 The table shows the number of rainy days in a town each month.

Jan	Feb	Mar	Apr	May	Jun	Jul	Aug	Sep	Oct	Nov	Dec
12	7	8	14	16	10	5	2	2	8	5	3

Find a the range
      b the mode
      c the median.

7 Lizi breeds dogs.

The bar chart shows the number of puppies born to each dog.

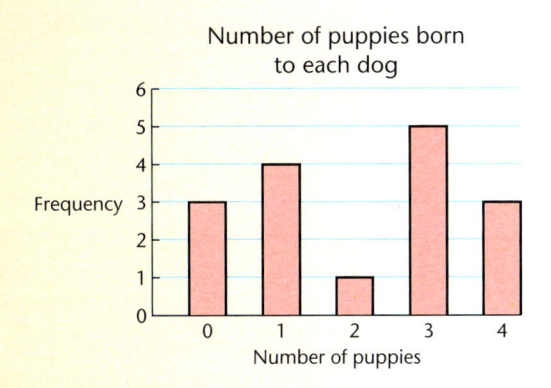

a Work out the range in the number of puppies born.
b Find the modal number of puppies born.
c Work out the median number of puppies born.

8 The pictogram shows the number of burglaries in each three-month period in a town.

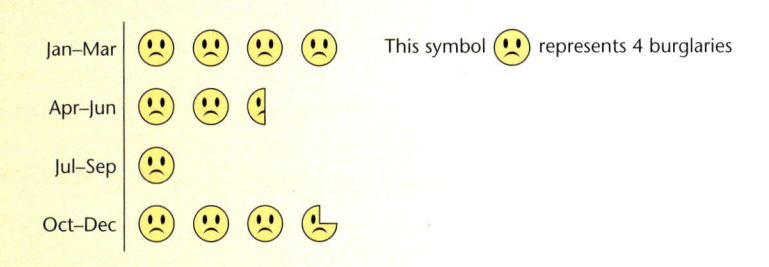

This symbol 🙁 represents 4 burglaries

a Work out the highest number of burglaries in a three-month period.
b Work out the lowest number of burglaries in a three-month period.
c Write down the range.
d Which three-month period has the modal number of burglaries?

9 There are 20 students in a class.
The stem-and-leaf diagram shows the number of half-days that they were absent last term.

Number of half-days absent   Key 1|6 means 16

```
0 | 0 0 0 0 1 1 4 4 9
1 | 0 0 1 2 7 7 8
2 | 2 5 6
3 | 5
```

> The modal number is the number of half-day absences that occurs most often.
>
> You need the number of half-day absences for the middle student of 20 students.

a Work out the range of the number of half-days absent.
b Find the modal number of half-days absent.
c Find the median for the number of half-days absent.

10 A children's charity has a telephone help line. The stem-and-leaf diagram shows the number of calls made each day in June.

Number of calls   Key 1|7 means 17 calls

```
0 | 7 9 9 9
1 | 0 0 1 2 7 7 8 9 9
2 | 0 1 1 5 6 6 6 6 8 9
3 | 0 1 2 2 3 3 5
```

a Work out the range.
b Write down the mode.
c What is the median number of calls during the month?

5.6 The mean from an ungrouped frequency table

You can find the mean from a frequency table but it needs to be done in an organised way.

Example 8

The table shows the marks out of 5 scored by students in a test.
Find the mean mark.

Maths marks in a test

Mark	Frequency
1	2
2	8
3	11
4	6
5	3
Total: 30	

Maths marks in a test

Mark	Frequency	Frequency x mark
1	2	2
2	8	16
3	11	33
4	6	24
5	3	15
	Total: 30	Total: 90

The sum of all the marks is 90. There are 30 students so the mean mark is 90 ÷ 30 = 3

> To find the mean of these marks, first you need to add up all the marks. It is easiest to do this in stages.
> The table shows that there are 2 lots of 1 mark, so these add up to 2. There are 8 lots of 2 marks, so the 2s add up to 8 × 2 = 16.
> Add another column to the table so that you can keep track of your work as you go down the table.

Exam practice 5F

1 Some students gathered this information about themselves.

Number of children in each family	Frequency	Frequency × number of children
1	8	
2	12	
3	4	
4	2	

> The mean = (sum of all the values) ÷ (number of values)

a Copy the table and complete the third column.
b Find the mean number of children per family.

2 Ellie counted the number of people queuing at each checkout in a supermarket.
She did this every five minutes. The table shows her results.

Number of people queuing at a supermarket checkout	Frequency	Frequency × number of people
1	6	
2	5	
3	2	
4	2	

a How many checkouts did she count?
b Copy the table and complete the third column.
c Find the mean number of people queuing.

3 Mark tossed three coins several times and wrote down the number of heads that showed at each toss.
His results are shown in the table.

Number of heads obtained when three coins are tossed	Frequency	Frequency × number of heads
0	4	
1	7	
2	16	
3	3	

Remember that $4 \times 0 = 0$.

a How many times did Mark toss the coin?
b Copy the table and complete the third column.
c Find the mean number of heads per toss.

4 The table shows the number of passengers in some cars.

Number of passengers	Number of cars (frequency)	Frequency × number of passengers
0	10	
1	15	
2	6	
3	7	
4	2	

a Copy the table and complete the third column.
b Write down the total number of cars.
c Work out the mean.

5 Some students emptied their pockets and counted how many one pound coins they had. The bar chart shows the result.

Number of £1 coins

The bar chart shows that 2 students had no £1 coins, 5 had one £1 coin, and so on.

You can list the value for each bar:
2 students had no £1 coins = £0
5 students each had one £1 coin = £5
10 students each had two £1 coins = £20
When you have listed all the values you can add them up.

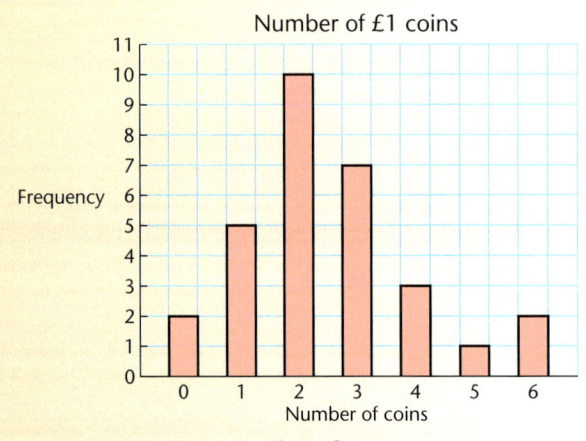

a How many students were there?
b What is the total value of the one pound coins?
c If the total sum of money was shared out equally among the students how much would each student have?

You need to divide your answer to part **b** by your answer to part **a**.

6 Tim breeds cats.
   The frequency polygon shows the number of kittens born to each cat.

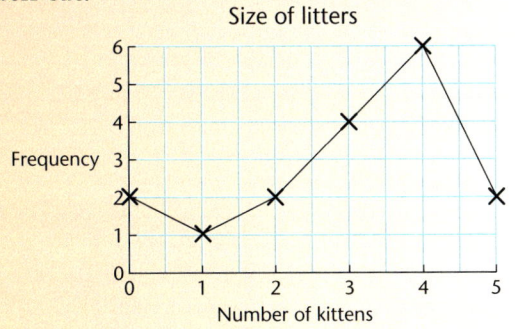

   Size of litters

   a Use the information to copy and fill in this table.

Number of kittens	Frequency	Number of kittens × frequency

   b Find the mean number of kittens born to a cat.

7 Chloe recorded the time she waited for a bus on 11 mornings. These are her results.

   Waiting time   Key 1|3 means 13 minutes
   0 | 1 2 3 5 5 7
   1 | 1 3 5 5
   2 | 2

   Work out the mean time.

   Start by listing these numbers: e.g. 1, 2, 3, 5, 5, 7, 11, and so on.

8 These are some test marks.

   Test mark   Key 1|3 means 13 marks
   0 | 5 6 6 8 9
   1 | 1 5 8 8
   2 | 4

   Work out the mean mark.

5.7 Range, mode and median from grouped frequency tables

We do not know the value of individual items when data is grouped. This means that we cannot find exact values for the range, the mode or the median.
For grouped data, we use these measures.

*These groups are also called **class intervals**.*

$$\text{estimated range} = \begin{array}{c}\text{highest value of}\\ \text{the top group}\end{array} - \begin{array}{c}\text{lowest value of}\\ \text{the bottom group}\end{array}$$

modal group = group with the largest number of values

We can also find the group that contains the median.

Example 9

Forty-five boxes of oranges were examined and the number of bad oranges in each box was counted. The results are shown in this table.

Number of bad oranges in a box	0–4	5–9	10–14	15–19
Frequency	29	11	4	1

a   Estimate the range.
b   Write down the modal group.
c   Which group contains the median?

a   19 oranges
b   0–4 oranges
c   There are 45 boxes. $\frac{45+1}{2} = 23$, so the middle box is the 23rd. The median is in the group 0–4.

> The highest value of the top group is 19. The lowest value of the bottom group is 0. The estimated range is 19 − 0.

> The group with the largest frequency.

> There are 29 boxes in the first group, so the 23rd is in this group.

Exam practice 5G

1   The table shows the result of a survey among 100 students on the amount of money each of them spent in the school tuck shop on one particular day.

Amount (pence)	0–49	50–99	100–149	150–200
Frequency	25	16	38	21

a   Find the range.
b   Write down the modal group.
c   Which class interval contains the median?

2   The table shows the value of houses sold in the last 6 months by an estate agent.

Value of house sold (£1000)	Frequency
10–49	2
50–99	8
100–149	6
150–199	4
200–400	2

a   Find the range.
b   Write down the modal group.
c   Which class interval contains the median?

> Show your working, even if you can find the median in your head.

3 This table shows the weekly earnings of the workforce in a factory.

Weekly earnings, £	150–200	201–250	251–300	301–350	351–400
Frequency	48	59	62	22	6

a Write down the size of the workforce.
b Find the range.
c Write down the modal group.
d Which class interval contains the median?

4 The table shows the daily number of rejects on a production line in a factory.

Number of rejects	0–5	6–10	11–15	16–20	21–25	26–30
Frequency	15	19	8	13	7	3

a How many days does this data cover?
b Find the range.
c Write down the modal group.
d Which class interval contains the median?

5 A group of students were asked how much money they had with them.
The results are shown in the table.

Amount (pence)	0–49	50–99	100–149	150–199	200–250
Frequency	5	12	12	16	9

a Find the range.
b Write down the modal group.
c Which class interval contains the median?

6 The table shows the numbers of words in each line of one page of a novel.

Number of words	1–3	4–6	7–9	10–12	13–15
Frequency	3	7	17	11	3

a Find the range.
b Write down the modal group.
c Which class interval contains the median?

7 The bar chart shows the number of defective components per crate in a delivery to a factory.

No. of defective components delivered

[Bar chart: Frequency on y-axis (0 to 12), Number of defective components per crate on x-axis. Bars: 0–2: 10; 3–5: 7; 6–8: 2; 9–11: 2]

a Find the range.
b Write down the modal group.
c Which group contains the median number of defective components?

ICT task
Use an internet search engine to find prices of one brand of MP3 player in different online shops. You will need at least five different prices.
Enter the prices you have found into a spreadsheet.
Use your spreadsheet to find:
- the range of prices
- the median price
- the mean price.

5.8 Finding the mean of a grouped frequency distribution

The estimated mean value of a grouped frequency distribution is given by

$$\frac{\text{sum of all (frequency} \times \text{mid-interval value)}}{\text{sum of frequencies}}$$

Example 10

This grouped frequency table shows the heights of 80 five-year-olds.

Height, h cm	Frequency
$90 \leqslant h < 95$	3
$95 \leqslant h < 100$	9
$100 \leqslant h < 105$	18
$105 \leqslant h < 110$	29
$110 \leqslant h < 115$	21
	Total: 80

Add two columns to the table: one to list the mid-interval values and one to list the frequency × mid-interval values.

Estimate the mean height.

Height, h cm	Frequency	Mid-interval value	Frequency × mid-interval value
$90 \leq h < 95$	3	92.5	277.5
$95 \leq h < 100$	9	97.5	877.5
$100 \leq h < 105$	18	102.5	1845
$105 \leq h < 110$	29	107.5	3117.5
$110 \leq h < 115$	21	112.5	2362.5
	Total: 80		Total: 8480

The mid-interval value for the first group is $(90 + 95) \div 2 = 92.5$. Use 92.5 cm as an estimate for the height of every child in this group. The estimated total height of all the children in this group is 3×92.5 cm = 277.5 cm.

The total height of all 80 children is estimated as 8480 cm
$\frac{8480}{80} = 106$ so the mean height is approximately 106 cm.

Exam practice 5H

1. Jake asked 100 pupils how much they spent on snacks today. His results are shown in the table.

Amount (pence)	Frequency
0–24	22
25–49	15
50–74	42
75–99	21

Find an estimate for the mean amount of money spent.

Copy the table and add two columns so that it is like the table above.
Each mid-interval value is the sum of the extreme values divided by 2.
So the mid-interval value of the 25–49 group is $(25 + 49) \div 2 = 37$.

2. Fifty boxes of tomatoes were examined and the number of bad tomatoes in each box was counted. The results are shown in the table.

Number of bad tomatoes per box	Frequency
0–4	35
5–9	10
10–14	4
15–19	1

Find an estimate for the mean number of bad tomatoes per box.

You need to make a table like the one in the example.

3. Ambulance response times to 999 calls are given in this table.

Response time, t minutes	$5 \leq t < 10$	$10 \leq t < 15$	$15 \leq t < 20$	$20 \leq t < 25$	$25 \leq t < 30$
Frequency	3	6	27	18	6

Find an estimate for the mean response time.

Take care! This table gives the groups going across. Either add two rows for mid-interval values and frequency × mid-interval values under the table or make a new table with the groups going down.

4 Twenty seeds were planted.
Five weeks later, the heights of the seedlings were measured.
The results are shown in the table.

Height, h cm	Frequency
$1 \leq h < 4$	2
$4 \leq h < 7$	5
$7 \leq h < 10$	10
$10 \leq h < 13$	3

Find an estimate for the mean height of the seedlings.

5 A group of people were asked to fill in a new benefit form and the time each person took was recorded. The results are shown in this frequency polygon.

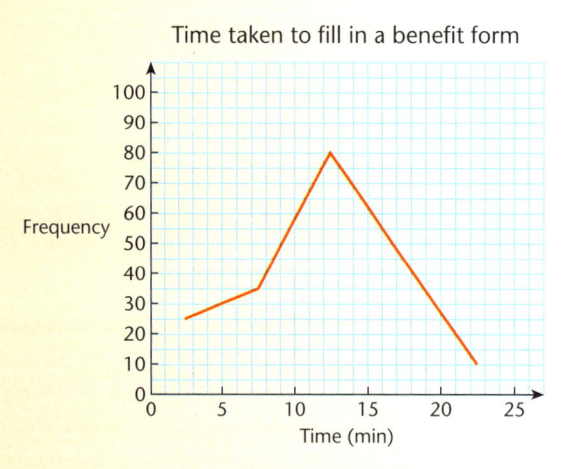

Time taken to fill in a benefit form

a How many people were asked to complete the form?
b Copy and complete this table.

Mid-interval value, (minutes)	Frequency	Frequency × mid-interval value
2.5	25	62.5
7.5	35	
	Total:	Total:

c Find an estimate for the mean time taken to complete this form.

6 This table shows the times taken by a group of painters to complete a job.

Time, t minutes	Number of painters
$0 \leq t < 5$	6
$5 \leq t < 10$	9
$10 \leq t < 15$	4
$15 \leq t < 20$	1

  a Find the range.
  b Write down the modal class.
  c Write down the class interval that contains the median time.
  d Estimate the mean.

7 This frequency table shows the heights of the 29 students in a class.

Height, h cm	$148 \leq h < 150$	$150 \leq h < 152$	$152 \leq h < 154$	$154 \leq h < 156$	$156 \leq h < 158$
Frequency	2	5	8	9	5

  a Find the range.
  b Write down the modal class.
  c Which class interval contains the median height?
  d Estimate the mean.

Class discussion

Which of the mean, median or mode will be the most useful in the following situations?
1 You want to know if you are taller or shorter than most women.
2 The school shop sells several different items.
  You need to buy more stock and do not want to run out of the most popular item.
3 You have some information about the temperature in Florida in February.
  You need to decide what clothes to take with you for a 10-day holiday to Florida in February.
4 You want an idea of the price you will have to pay for an inkjet photo printer.

Summary of key points

- The mode is the value that occurs most often.
- The range is the difference between the highest and lowest values.
- There are three different kinds of averages:
  arithmetic mean or **mean**, **median** and **mode**
- You find the mean by adding all the values then dividing this sum by the number of values.
- The median is the middle value when all the values have been arranged in order. When there are two middle values, the median is halfway between them.
- You can find which value is the middle one by adding 1 to the number of values and dividing by 2.
- For grouped data,
  - the range is highest value of top group − lowest value of the bottom group
  - the modal class is the class with the highest frequency
  - the mean is estimated as

$$\frac{\text{sum of all (mid-interval values} \times \text{frequency)}}{\text{total frequency}}$$

Most students who get GRADE E or above can:
- find the mean, median and mode from an ungrouped frequency table.

Most students who get GRADE C can also:
- find the mean from a grouped frequency table and identify the class containing the median.

Glossary

Arithmetic mean	the sum of a set of values divided by the number of values
Average	any one of the mean, mode or median
Class interval	range of continuous data
Frequency table	a table listing the possible values or groups of values, and their frequencies
Mean	the sum of a set of values divided by the number of values
Median	the middle value after a set of values have been arranged in order of size
Mid-interval value	the middle value in a group or class
Mode	the value or values that occur most often
Range	the difference between the largest and smallest value

6 Two-way tables and scatter graphs

This chapter will show you:
✓ how to get information from a two-way table
✓ how to draw a scatter graph
✓ how to judge whether there is a relationship between two sets of information

Before you start you need to know:
✓ how to scale axes and plot points on a graph
✓ how to read values from scaled axes

6.1 Two-way tables

See Chapter 2 for more information on two-way tables.

Two-way tables are used to give two groups of related information.

Example 1

This two-way table shows the grades of a group of students in two GCSE modules.

GCSE in June 2005

	D	E	F	G	U
Module 1	20	22	10	2	9
Module 3	5	3	2	0	1

a How many students got grade E in Module 1?
b How many students got grade D in Module 3?

Look along the row labelled 'Module 1' until you get to the column headed 'E'.

Look along the row labelled 'Module 3' until you get to the column headed 'D'.

a 22
b 5

Exam practice 6A

1 Use the two-way table in the example above to find
   a the number of students who sat Module 3 in June 2005
   b the number of students sitting Module 1, who got grades D to F.

   Look along the row labelled 'Module 3' and add up all the numbers in that row.

2 The table shows students in Year 10 with and without jobs.

Students in Year 10

	Job	No job
Boys	32	25
Girls	28	21

a How many girls have jobs?
b How many boys do not have jobs?
c How many students do not have a job?

'Students' means boys and girls, so you need to find the number of boys who do not have a job and the number of girls who do not have a job. Then you need to add these two numbers.

3 The table shows people in a group with either long or short hair.

People in a group

	Long hair	Short hair
Men	5	21
Women	16	8

a How many men have long hair?
b How many women have short hair?
c How many people have long hair?

4 The table shows the number of students on a field trip with and without a pen.

Students on a field trip

	Have a pen	Without a pen
Boys	15	8
Girls	17	4

a How many boys have a pen?
b How many girls are without a pen?
c How many students are without a pen?

5 The cars and lorries passing King Street were stopped and checked. The table shows the result.

Vehicles passing King Street

	Satisfactory lights	Defective lights
Cars	73	7
Lorries	32	6

a How many cars had defective lights?
b How many lorries did not have defective lights?
c How many vehicles did not have defective lights?
d How many vehicles were checked?

> Read questions slowly. Read them several times to check that you understand what you are asked to find.

6 This table shows the grades obtained by a group of students.

GCSE Grades Nov. 2005

	C	D	E	F	G	U
Module 1	8	21	24	8	3	9
Module 3	7	6	3	3	0	1

a How many students sat Module 1?
b How many students sat Module 3 and got a grade E?
c How many students sat Module 1 and got either grade D or grade E?

7 The table shows last year's Key Stage 3 results for a group.

Key Stage 3 Levels

	4	5	6
Boys	12	28	25
Girls	12	27	30

a How many students were at Level 6?
b How many boys were at Level 5 or higher?
c How many girls were lower than Level 5?

'Level 5 **or higher**' means 'Levels 5 **and** 6'.

8 The table shows the grades in a maths test and in a science test.

Maths Grade

Science Grade

	A	B	C
A	2	5	4
B	6	7	3
C	7	5	9

a Find the number of students who got grade B or better in the maths test.
b How many students got the same grade in both tests?
c How many students got a higher grade in the science test than in the maths test?

All the students in the column headed 'B' got a grade B in maths. All the students in the column headed 'A' got better than a grade B in maths.

Find the sum of the numbers in the diagonal from 2 to 9.

Mini coursework task

Adam read that girls do better than boys at GCSE.
He decided to test this.
● Write down a hypothesis for him to test.
● Design a two-way table so that Adam can collect the information.

6.2 Using and plotting scatter graphs

A **scatter graph** is a way of illustrating information from a two-way table.

Example 2

The table shows the height and shoe size of eight women.

Woman

	A	B	C	D	E	F	G	H
Height (cm)	160	166	174	158	166	161	168	170
Shoe size (continental)	36	38	40	37	40	38	39	42

a Draw a scatter graph for this data.
b Jan said that 'Tall people have larger feet than short people.'
   Use your scatter graph to test this **hypothesis**.

a

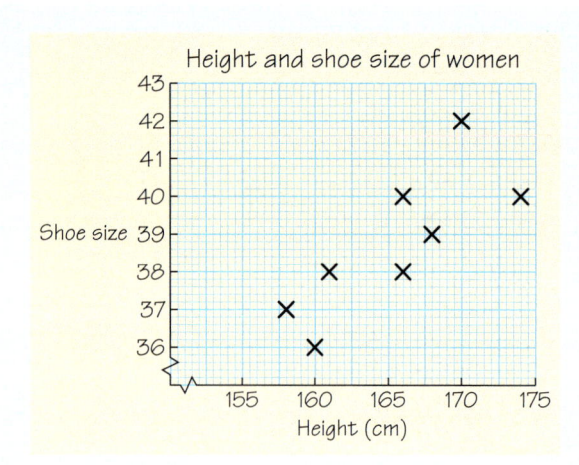

Height and shoe size of women

[Scatter graph with Shoe size (36–43) on vertical axis and Height (cm) (155–175) on horizontal axis, showing crosses plotted for each woman.]

> Draw a grid. Scale the height axis (the horizontal axis) from 155 to 175 and the shoe size axis (the vertical axis) from 36 to 43.

> Plot one point to represent each woman.
> The coordinates for woman A are 160 across and 36 up.

b The scatter graph shows that taller women tend to have larger feet.

> The statement describes a tendency. It will not always be true.

Exam practice 6B

1 Use the scatter graph in Example 2 to answer these questions.
   a How many of the women were taller than 165 cm?
   b How many women take a shoe size smaller than 38?

> Find the grid line marking a height of 165 cm. The crosses to the right of this line represent heights greater than 165 cm.

> You will find it easier to count if you place a ruler along the horizontal grid line through size 38.

2 This graph shows the age and price of some second-hand cars. The cars are all small with similar engine sizes.

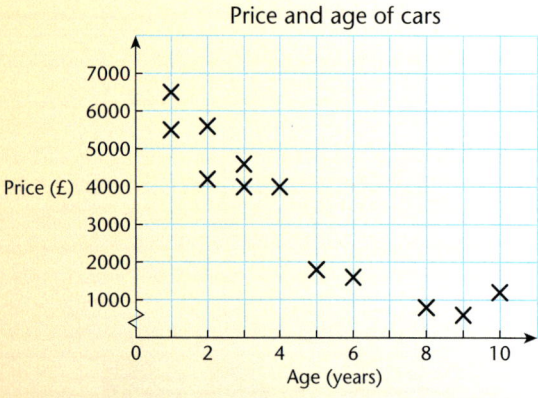

Price and age of cars

[Scatter graph with Price (£) from 1000 to 7000 on vertical axis and Age (years) from 0 to 10 on horizontal axis.]

   a How many of these cars cost more than £3000?
   b How many cars are more than 7 years old?
   c James says that 'The price of a second-hand car gets lower as the age increases.'
      Is James correct? Explain your answer.

3 Ashe saw this headline in a paper,
   'Tall children are cleverer than short children.'
   He did not believe it, so he did some research.
   Ashe collected data from a group of Year 11 students.
   The scatter graph shows his results.

Chapter 6 Two-way tables and scatter graphs   79

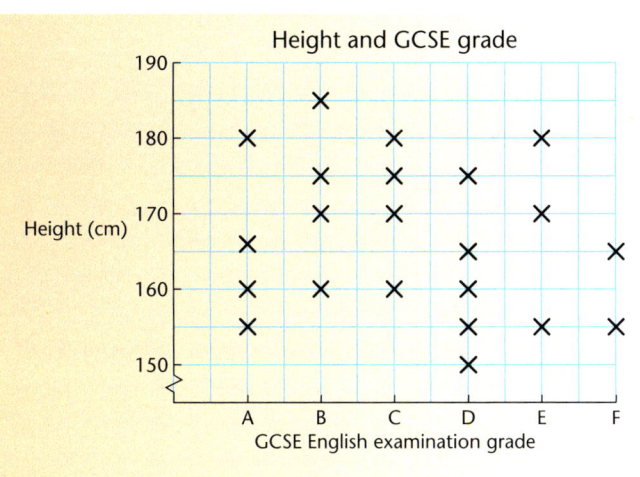

a Does this scatter graph support the hypothesis that tall children do better at GCSE than short children? Explain your answer.

b How many students shorter than 165 cm got grades A or B?

> You need the number of crosses below the 165 grid line that are on the grade A and grade B lines.

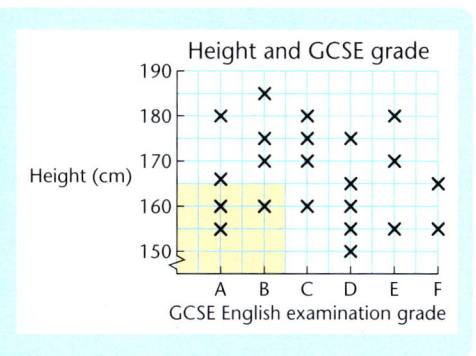

4 The scatter graph shows the marks of a group of students in a coursework task and in a written examination.

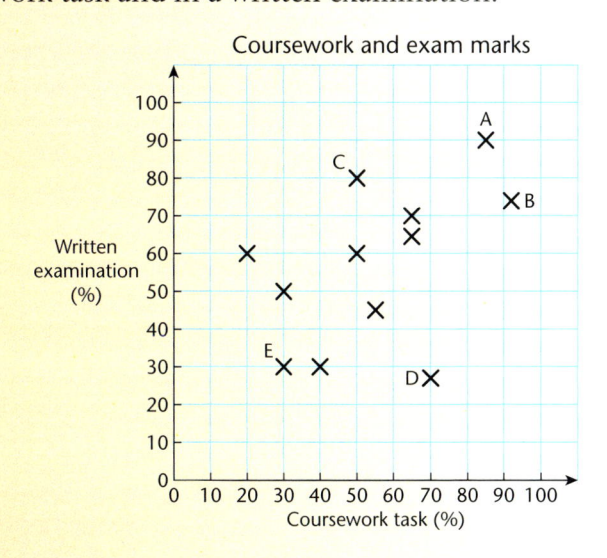

a Which letter refers to a student who got the highest mark on the coursework task?

b Which letter refers to the student who got the same mark for the coursework task and for the written examination?

c How many students are represented on the graph?

5 This table shows the number of rooms in twelve houses and the number of people living in each house.

Number of rooms	4	4	5	5	6	6	6	7	7	7	8	8
Number of people	3	5	2	1	6	3	4	3	4	5	2	6

a Show this information on a scatter graph.
  Use a scale of 1 cm for 1 unit on each axis.
b Ellie lives in a house with four other people.
  Is the house likely to have more than four rooms?

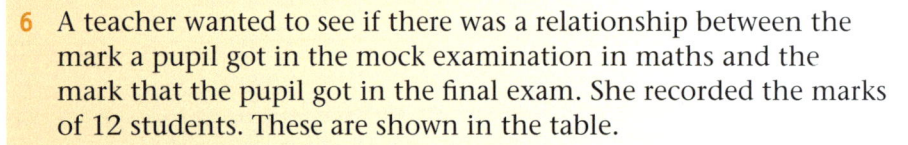

6 A teacher wanted to see if there was a relationship between the mark a pupil got in the mock examination in maths and the mark that the pupil got in the final exam. She recorded the marks of 12 students. These are shown in the table.

Mock mark	72	84	85	41	46	57	44	43	56	80	52	38
Final mark	84	73	77	53	62	54	55	56	48	66	72	50

a Draw a scatter diagram to show this data on a graph.
  Use 1 cm to represent 5 marks on both axes.
  Mark each axis from 30 to 90.
b Does your scatter diagram support the hypothesis that results in the mock exam give a good idea of the mark a student is likely to get in the final exam?
c Tyler got 66 in the mock but failed to take the final exam. Use the scatter graph to estimate what he might have scored in the final exam.

6.3 Line of best fit

The **line of best fit** is the straight line about which the points on the graph are evenly distributed.

This is the graph from Example 2. It shows the height and shoe size of 8 women. You can draw the line of best fit by eye.

There should be roughly the same number of points above the line as below it. This may mean that none of the points is on the line.

Chapter 6 Two-way tables and scatter graphs   81

Exam practice 6C

1. This scatter graph shows the number of bad oranges in a box after different delivery times. The line of best fit has been drawn on the graph.

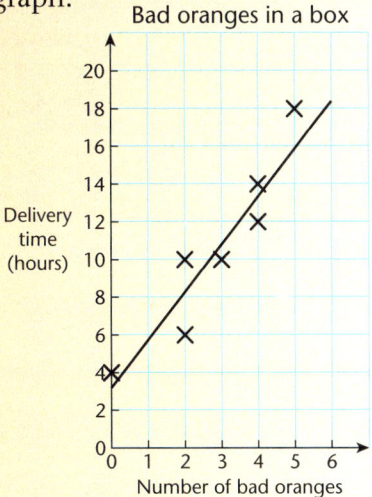

    Bad oranges in a box

    > Find 6 on the horizontal axis. Go from this point up to the line of best fit and then across to the vertical axis. Now read the value there.
    >
    > Make sure that you understand what each subdivision on the vertical scale represents. 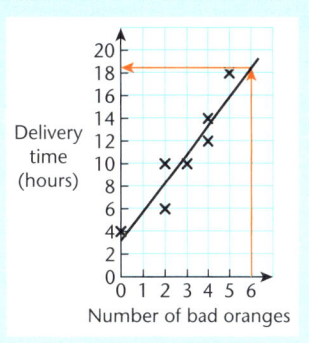

    One box contained 6 bad oranges.
    Use the diagram to estimate the delivery time for this box.

2. The scatter diagram shows data collected over eight years by a breeder of goldfish.

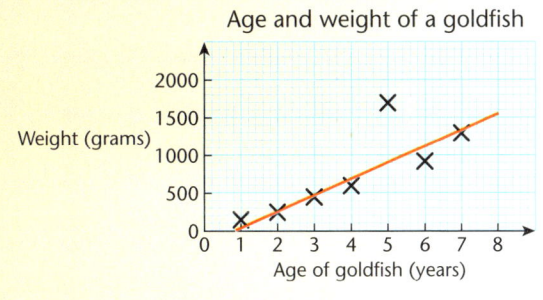

    Age and weight of a goldfish

    a Explain why one of the points is likely to have been plotted incorrectly.
    b Estimate the average weight of a five-year-old goldfish.

    > Look for a point that is much further away from the line than any other point. Use this point and describe its distance from the line as your reason in your explanation.

3. The graph shows the French and maths marks of 20 pupils in an end of term exam.

    Exam marks

    a Omar got 74 for maths and 68 for French.
    Add a cross to a copy of the scatter diagram to show Omar's marks.

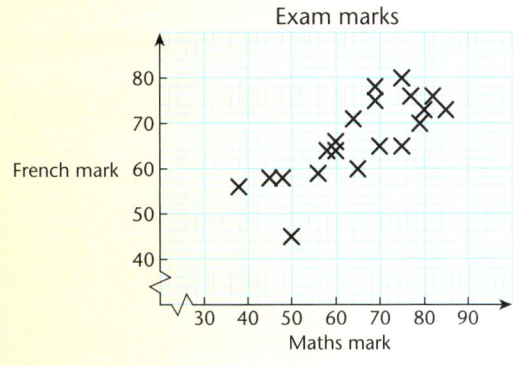

    > Make sure you know what each subdivision on the scales means.

b Draw a line of best fit for all 21 marks.

c Describe the relationship between the maths marks and the French marks.

d John is good at French.

Is he likely to be good at maths?

Explain your answer.

> Write a short sentence giving a reason based on your answer to part **c**.

e Ahmed got 65 for his French examination but was absent on the day of the maths examination.
Estimate his likely mark if he had taken the maths examination.

6.4 Correlation

Linear correlation means that the points are scattered about a straight line.
The closer the points are to the line, the stronger the correlation.

There are two types of correlation.

Positive **linear correlation** is when the line of best fit slopes upwards.

There is positive correlation in this graph. (It is the graph shown in 6.3.)

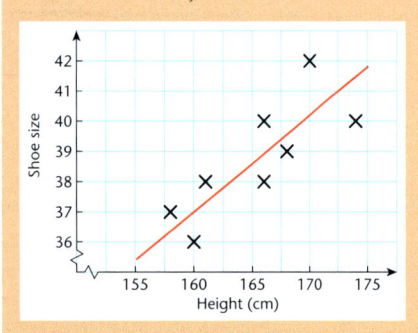

This means that shoe size tends to increase with a person's height.

Negative **linear correlation** is when the line of best fit slopes downwards.

There is negative correlation in this graph.

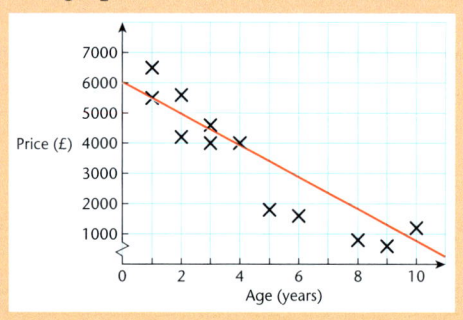

The graph shows the prices of some cars at different ages.
The value of a car goes down as it gets older.

When the points are close to the line, there is a **strong linear correlation**.

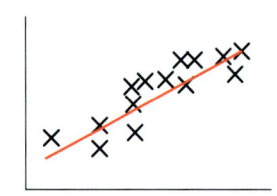

Strong positive correlation

When the points are loosely scattered about the line, there is **weak linear correlation**.

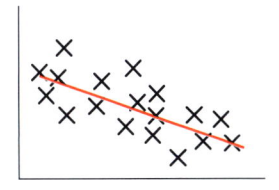

Weak negative correlation

Sometimes the points are so scattered that there is no obvious line.
There is **no linear correlation**.

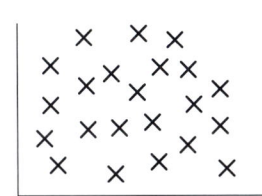

There is no obvious line of best fit in this diagram.

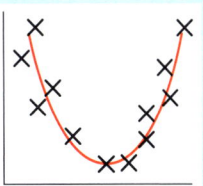

However the red curve shows there is a relationship. We say there is no **linear** correlation.

Exam practice 6D

1 This table shows the heights and weights of 10 people.

Height (cm)	150	152	155	158	158	160	163	165	170	175
Weight (kg)	56	62	69	64	57	62	68	66	65	74

a Plot this information as a scatter graph.
b Draw a line of best fit.
c Describe the relationship between height and weight.

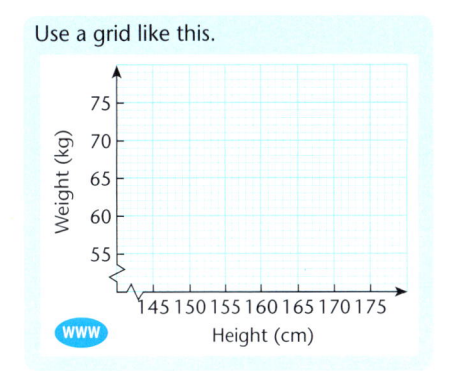

Use a grid like this.

2 This table shows the number of rooms in each of 15 houses and the number of people living in each house.

Number of rooms	3	4	4	5	5	5	6	6	6	6	7	7	7	8	8
Number of people	2	5	3	4	2	1	6	2	3	4	4	5	3	6	2

a Plot this information as a scatter graph.
b Draw a line of best fit on your scatter graph.
c Describe the relationship shown in the scatter graph.
d Use your scatter graph to estimate the number of rooms in a house with 7 people living in it.
e Describe how reliable your answer to part **d** is.
Explain your answer.

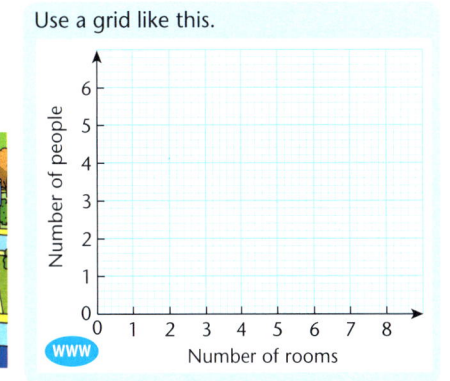

Use a grid like this.

f A data collection sheet looked like this:

House						
Number of rooms in the house and number of people in the house						

Give **one** reason why this is not suitable.

3 This table shows the number of pencils and the number of exercise books that each of 10 pupils have with them in a maths lesson.

Number of pencils	2	3	3	5	6	6	12	15	20	24
Number of exercise books	4	0	5	3	1	4	6	2	1	6

a Plot this data as a scatter graph.
b Give one reason why it is not sensible to draw a line of best fit on your diagram.
c A questionnaire contained this question.

> HOW MANY BOOKS ARE IN YOUR BAG?

Give **one** reason why this question is not suitable.

Use a grid like this.

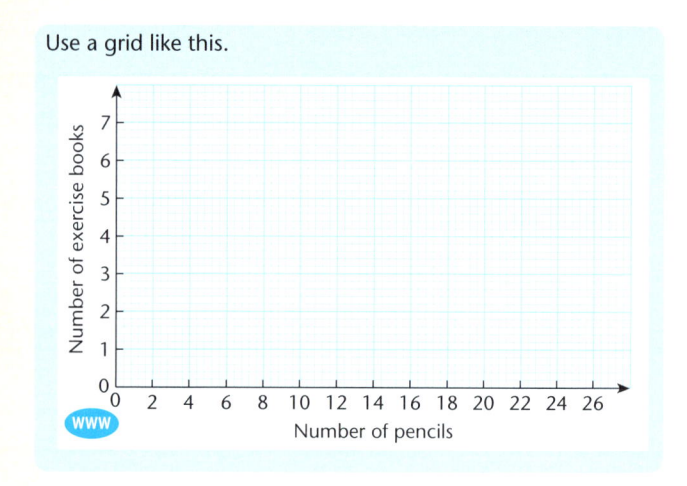

(scatter graph grid: Number of exercise books 0–7 vs Number of pencils 0–26)

4 Match each sentence with the letter of the scatter graph that you think best matches the relationship. Describe the correlation (if any) in each case.
  a The number of pages and the number of advertisements in a newspaper.
  b The length and width of a cucumber.
  c The weight of tomatoes produced by a tomato plant and its height.
  d The age of a child and their best 100 m running time.
  e The score on each dice when a red dice and a blue dice are thrown together.
  f The number of days a pupil is away from school and the number of days when that pupil is late in handing in coursework.

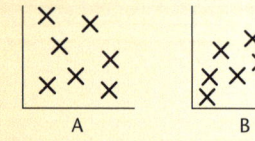

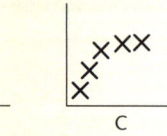

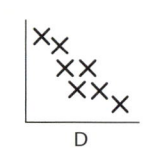

A   B   C   D

5 Fahed collected this data about the village he lived in.

Year	1965	1970	1975	1980	1985	1990	1995	2000
Population	100	150	300	550	400	180	400	250
Number of fish in the village pond	20	30	50	80	70	40	60	40

a Plot the population and number of fish as a scatter graph.

b Fahed looked at the scatter graph for the data and said 'If we put a lot more fish in the pond, we will get more people living here.'
Fahed is not correct.
Explain why he is wrong.

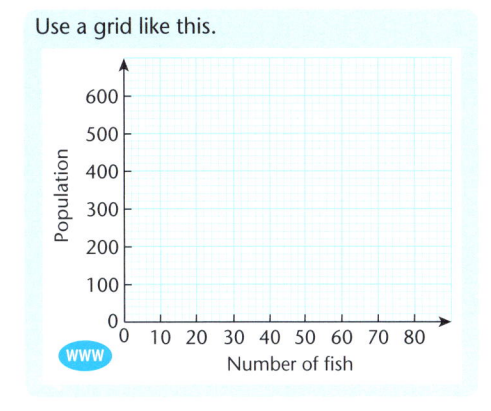

Use a grid like this.

Summary of key points

- Two-way tables are used to show different aspects of a set of data.
- Scatter graphs are used to show data when you have two pieces of information about a person or an object.
- If the points on a scatter graph look as if they may be scattered about a line, you can judge by eye where this line is and draw it – it is called the line of best fit.
- Correlation describes how close the points are to the line of best fit.

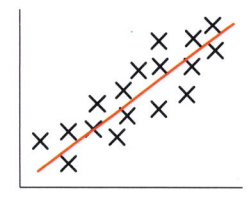

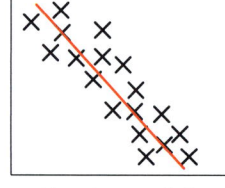

Positive correlation   Negative correlation

- If there is no obvious line of best fit, there is no linear correlation.
- No linear correlation does not mean that there is no relationship.

Most students who get GRADE E or above can:
- get information from a two-way table.

Most students who get GRADE C can also:
- draw a line of best fit and describe the correlation between two sets of data.

Glossary

Correlation	relationship between two quantities
Hypothesis	statement that may or may not be true
Linear	description of a straight line
Line of best fit	straight line drawn on a scatter graph to best fit the scatter of the points
Scatter graph	points plotted on a graph to show two sets of information
Two-way table	table giving two or more groups of information

7 Probability 1

This chapter will show you:
- ✓ the meaning of special words used in probability
- ✓ how to find the probability that an event happens
- ✓ how to find the number of times you can expect an event to happen
- ✓ how to use an experiment to estimate probability

Before you start you need to know:
- ✓ the meaning of fractions
- ✓ what an even number, an odd number and a prime number is
- ✓ how to find one quantity as a fraction of another
- ✓ how to simplify a fraction
- ✓ how to multiply a whole number by a fraction
- ✓ what the cards are in an ordinary pack of 52 playing cards

7.1 Probability

Probability is about measuring the likelihood that something might happen.

Some things cannot happen.
For example, it is impossible that you will take a pen out of a bag that has only pencils in it.

Some things are certain to happen.
For example, it is certain that the sun will rise tomorrow.

Some things may or may not happen.
For example, when you flip a coin, it may or may not show a head.

Class discussion

Decide if each event is impossible, may happen, or is certain to happen.
1. A slice of toast will land butter side down when dropped.
2. You will go out next weekend.
3. When you throw an ordinary dice it will score 7.
4. The next sweet in a tube of boiled sweets is broken.
5. It will get dark tonight.
6. The next vehicle to pass the school gate will be a coach.
7. You will have homework tonight.
8. When you throw a dice it will score six.
9. When you take a card from an ordinary pack of playing cards it will be a black card.
10. You will see a shooting star if you look at the sky tonight.

7.2 Outcomes of an experiment

An **experiment** is something you do without knowing what will happen.
The act of throwing a dice is an experiment.

An **outcome** or an **event** is what happens when you do an experiment.
If you throw an ordinary dice, one possible outcome is a score of 4.

All possible outcomes are all the events that can happen when you do an experiment.
When you throw an ordinary dice, the possible outcomes are 1, 2, 3, 4, 5 or 6.

Did you know

that most people think that their chance of winning the lottery is better if they choose numbers that are not next to each other? It isn't. The chance of winning with the numbers 1, 2, 3, 4, 5, 6 is exactly the same as with any other set of six numbers such as 4, 12, 25, 29, 31, 43.

Exam practice 7A

1. A coin is flipped. List all the possible outcomes.

   Assume it lands flat.

2. This spinner is spun. List all the possible outcomes.

   It cannot land on a point.

3. One disc is taken from a bag containing 1 red, 1 blue and 1 yellow disc.
   Write down all the possible outcomes.

4. One number is taken from the first ten counting numbers.
   Write down a list of all the possible outcomes.

   The counting numbers are 1, 2, 3, 4,…

5. A box contains 1 red, 1 yellow, 1 blue, 1 brown, 1 black and 1 green crayon.
   Write down a list of all the possible outcomes when one crayon is taken from this box.

6. One item is selected from a bag containing 1 packet of chewing gum, 1 packet of boiled sweets and 1 bar of chocolate. Write down a list of all the possible outcomes.

7. A bag contains one 2p coin, one 5p coin, one 20p coin and one 50p coin.
   One coin is taken from the bag.
   Write down a list of all the possible outcomes.

8. One number is chosen from the first 5 prime numbers.
   a Write down the number of possible outcomes.
   b Write down a list of all the possible outcomes

   The prime numbers are 2, 3, 5,… A prime number has exactly two factors, itself and 1.

9. An even number is chosen from the first 10 counting numbers.
   Write down a list of all the possible outcomes.

10. Rebecca picks out one card from an ordinary pack of 52 playing cards.
    Write down the number of possible choices she has.

    Read the question carefully. Make sure you understand what you are asked to find.

7.3 The probability scale

The probability (or **chance**) that something might happen is somewhere between impossible and certain. You can measure probability on a scale going from 'impossible' at one end to 'certain' at the other end. In between you can use words such as 'likely' and 'unlikely'.

Equally likely or **evens** can be used to describe the probability that something is as likely as not to happen.
For example, when you flip a coin it is equally likely to land on heads or tails.
The probability that it will show a head can be described as evens.

This is a probability scale using words.

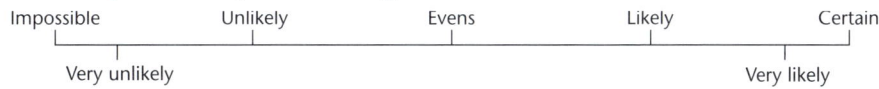

Impossible — Very unlikely — Unlikely — Evens — Likely — Very likely — Certain

The words **fair** or **unbiased** are used to describe coins, dice and spinners that have equally likely outcomes.
A coin, dice or spinner is **biased** if one outcome is more likely than the others.

Example 1

Draw an arrow on the scale to show the probability of getting 4 when this fair spinner is spun.

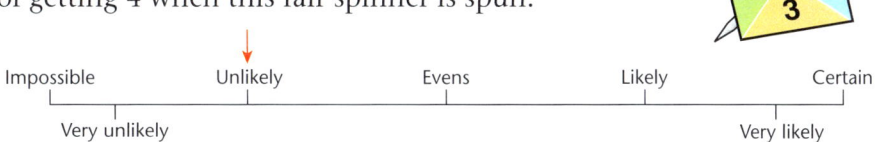

Impossible — Very unlikely — Unlikely (↓) — Evens — Likely — Very likely — Certain

Showing a 4 is only 1 out of 4 equally likely outcomes.
So the probability that it will show a four is unlikely.

Exam practice 7B

1 The probability of each of these events is shown with an arrow. Copy the scale and label each arrow to show which event it represents.

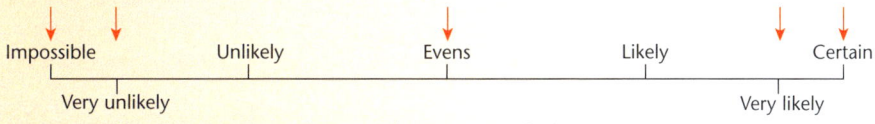

Impossible (↓↓) — Very unlikely — Unlikely — Evens (↓) — Likely — Very likely (↓↓) — Certain

   A An ordinary fair dice is thrown and shows a six.
   B A fair coin is flipped and shows a head.
   C An ordinary fair dice is rolled and shows a seven.
   D An ordinary fair dice is rolled and does not show a six.
   E This fair three-sided spinner lands on 1.

2 The probability of each of these events is shown with an arrow. Write down the number of the arrow which represents each event.

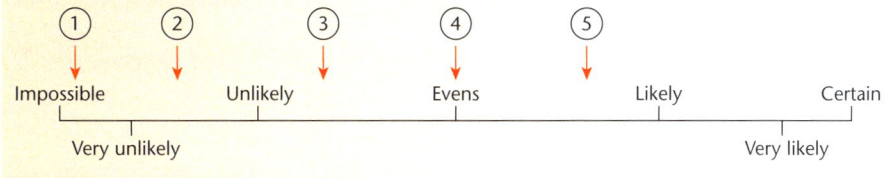

①↓ ②↓ ③↓ ④↓ ⑤↓

Impossible — Very unlikely — Unlikely — Evens — Likely — Very likely — Certain

One of the arrows is not needed.

   a A bag contains 1 red, 1 blue and 1 yellow disc. One disc is taken out of the bag at random and it is red.
   b A letter is chosen at random from the letters in the word MASTER. It is the letter M.
   c A card is taken at random from a full pack of ordinary playing cards. It is the ace of spades.
   d A letter is chosen from the letters in the word OUR. It is a vowel.

The phrase '**at random**' means that any one card is as likely to be picked as any other card.

The vowels are the letters : a, e, i, o, u.

A01 3 A bag contains one red disc and one blue disc. Is the chance of taking out a red disc the same as the chance of taking out a blue one? Give a reason for your answer.

Write down why you answered yes or no.

A01 4 An ordinary fair dice is rolled. Are the six different possible scores equally likely?
Write down a reason for your answer.

A01 5 A bag contains two red discs and one blue disc. One disc is chosen at random from the bag. Emma said that the chance that the disc is red is the same as the chance that it is blue.
Is Emma correct? Give a reason for your answer.

A01 6 Sally takes a disc at random out of a bag which contains 10 white discs and 10 green discs. Sally said 'The chance that it is a green disc is evens'. Was Sally correct?
Give a reason for your answer.

7.4 Calculating probabilities

The probability that an event happens is the fraction

$$\frac{\text{number of ways that the event can happen}}{\text{total number of equally likely outcomes}}$$

You can use this definition to work out probabilities.

Example 2

If you throw an ordinary fair dice, what is the probability of getting a four?

$$\frac{\text{number of ways that the event can happen}}{\text{total number of equally likely outcomes}} = \frac{1}{6}$$

The dice is fair so all outcomes are equally likely.

There is only one way of getting 4. There are 6 equally likely outcomes.

Example 3

One card is drawn at random from a pack of playing cards. Calculate the probability that it will be the ace of spades.

Probability of choosing the ace of spades =

$$\frac{\text{number of ways of picking the ace of spades}}{\text{number of ways of picking any card}} = \frac{1}{52}$$

The phrase '**at random**' means that any one card is as likely to be picked as any other.

There are 52 cards in a full pack. There is only one ace of spades.

The probability that an event is impossible is 0 because there is no possible outcome.

The probability that an event is certain is 1 because the only outcome is that event.

The probability that most events might happen is somewhere between 0 and 1.

You can now draw the probability scale using numbers instead of words.

0    $\frac{1}{4}$ $\frac{1}{2}$ $\frac{3}{4}$ 1

Exam practice 7C

1 The probability of each of these events is marked with an arrow. Copy the scale and label the arrow that represents each event.

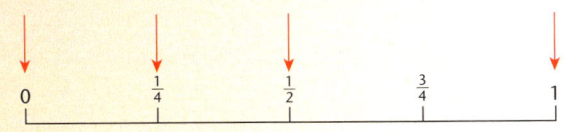

A Kay flips a fair coin. The coin shows a head.
B Brad rolls an ordinary fair dice. The dice shows 10.
C A bag contains 3 black marbles and 1 clear marble. Michelle takes one marble at random. The marble is clear.

One of the arrows is not needed.

2 The probability of each of these events is marked with an arrow. Write down the number of the arrow that represents each event.

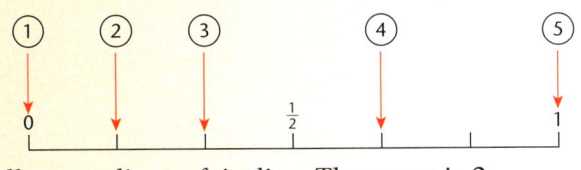

a Eleri rolls an ordinary fair dice. The score is 2.
b This fair spinner is spun. It shows a 2.
c This fair spinner is spun. It shows a 4.

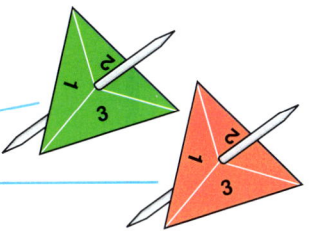

3 Here is a probability scale.

Copy the scale and put the letters **A**, **B** and **C** on your copy at the points which represent the following events.

A The probability of throwing a head with a fair coin.
B The probability of picking a red counter from a bag full of red counters.
C The probability of picking a white counter from a bag full of blue counters.

4 One letter is chosen at random from the letters in the word SALE. Write down the probability that it is A.

Give your answer as a fraction.

5 A pencil is chosen at random from a box containing 10 coloured pencils. Only one pencil is red.
Copy this probability scale and mark an arrow on it to show the probability of choosing a red pencil.

6 A number is chosen at random from the numbers 6, 7, 8. Write down the probability that it is an odd number.

7 Emma, Sue, Freda, Emily and Julie are chatting.
One of them is chosen at random.
Write down the probability that it is Emily.

8 A number is chosen at random from the numbers 7, 8, 9, 10, 11, 12, 13.
   Write down the probability that you can divide it exactly by 5.

9 400 raffle tickets are sold.
   Colin buys one ticket.
   Write down the probability that Colin will win first prize.

10 A bag contains only £1 coins. A coin is drawn at random.
   Write down the probability that it is a £1 coin.

11 A bag contains only 10 p and 20 p coins. A coin is drawn at random.
   Write down the probability that it is a pound coin.

> You must give a probability as a fraction or decimal between 0 and 1. Do not give your answers as odds or ratios.

7.5 Events that can happen in more than one way

Some events can happen in many ways.
For example, you can get an even number when a dice is rolled if it shows 2, 4 or 6.

Example 4

One card is picked at random from an ordinary pack of playing cards. What is the probability that it is an ace?

Probability of picking an ace =

$$\frac{\text{the number of ways of picking an ace}}{\text{number of ways of picking any card}} = \frac{4}{52} = \frac{1}{13}$$

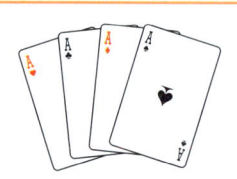

> There are 4 aces, so there are 4 ways in which an ace can be picked.
> Altogether there are 52 cards. Any one of these is equally likely to be picked.

Exam practice 7D

1 An ordinary dice is rolled.
   a Write down the number of different scores that are possible.
   b Calculate the probability of getting a score greater than 4.

> Simplify the fraction.

2 A lucky dip contains 50 boxes.
   Ten of them contain a prize. The rest are empty.
   Work out the probability of choosing a box that contains a prize.

3 A bag contains 3 white discs and 2 black discs.
   One disc is taken at random from the bag.
   Work out the probability that the disc is white.

   Probability that the disc is white
   $= \dfrac{\text{number of white discs in the bag}}{\text{total number of discs in the bag}}$

4 This fair spinner is spun.
   What is the probability that it shows an even number?

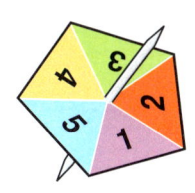

5 A number is chosen at random from the first 9 counting numbers.
   a Write down the number of ways of choosing an even number.
   b Work out the probability that an even number is chosen.

6 A number is picked at random from the numbers
         2, 3, 4, 5, 6, 7, 8, 9, 10, 11.
   a Write down the number of ways there are of doing this.
   b Work out the probability that a prime number is chosen.

   A prime number has no factors other than itself and 1.
   For example 2, 3 and 5 are prime numbers but 4 and 6 are not.

7 One card is taken at random from an ordinary pack of 52 playing cards.
   a Write down the number of ways there are of doing this.
   b Work out the probability that the card is
      i a king   ii a red card   iii a diamond.

   There are two red suits: hearts and diamonds.

8 One letter is chosen at random from the word BEGINNINGS.
   Work out the probability that it is
   a the letter N
   b the letter I
   c a vowel
   d one of the first five letters of the alphabet.

   The vowels are: a, e, i, o, u.

9 An ordinary six-sided dice is thrown.
   Work out the probability that the score is
   a greater than 3
   b at least 3
   c less than 3.

   Greater than 3 means 4, 5, or 6.

   At least 3 means 3 or more.

10 Copy the scale and mark the probability of each of these events with an arrow and label your arrow.

   0   1

   A Ben rolls an ordinary fair dice. The score is even.
   B Janet rolls an ordinary fair dice. The score is a greater than 2.
   C Darren rolls an ordinary fair dice. The number showing is less than 3.

11 Holly has a bag with 10 counters in it. There are 3 red counters, 1 blue counter and 6 black counters.
Holly takes one counter from the bag at random.
Copy the scale and mark the probability of each of these events with an arrow and label the arrow.

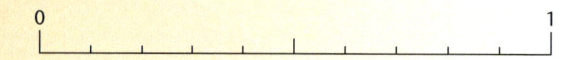

0 ————————————— 1

A The counter is blue.

B The counter is red.

C The counter is black.

12 The probability of each of these events is marked with an arrow.
Write down the number of the arrow that represents each event.

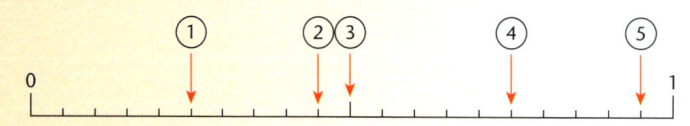

(Arrows 1, 2, 3, 4, 5 on a 0 to 1 scale)

a Debbie takes a disc out at random from a bag containing 3 red discs and 3 white discs.
The disc is white.

b Paul takes one number at random from the counting numbers 1 to 20.
The number is less than 10.

c Gordon has 2 red cards and 6 black cards.
Jim selects one card at random. It is a black card.

d This spinner is spun and it shows a number greater than 3.

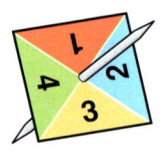

There are more arrows than you need.

13 400 raffle tickets were sold. There was one prize.

a Work out the probability that the number on the winning ticket was greater than 300.

b Keith bought 10 tickets.
Find the probability that Keith wins the prize.

Assume that the tickets are numbered 1 to 400.

14 One child is chosen at random from a group of 30 boys and girls.
Ten of these children are left-handed.

a Calculate the probability that the child chosen is left-handed.

b Raj said 'The probability that a girl is chosen is $\frac{1}{2}$.'
Write down a reason why Raj may be wrong.

7.6 Using frequency diagrams

Possible outcomes can be listed in tables or other diagrams.

Exam practice 7E

1. This table shows the number of computers in 20 houses.

Number of computers	Frequency
0	3
1	5
2	10
3	2

   One of these houses is chosen at random.

   Work out the probability that there are 2 computers in this house.

   > You need to find the number of houses in the table that have 2 computers and the total number of houses.

2. This stem-and-leaf diagram shows the marks scored by students in a test.

   ```
   Marks                    1|4 means 14
   1 | 4 4 5
   2 | 0 4 5 6 7 7
   3 | 0 1 2 3 3 4 4 5 8 9
   ```

   a. How many marks are shown in the diagram?

   b. One of these marks is chosen at random.
      Work out the probability that it is more than 20.

3. This bar chart shows how 28 students travelled to college.

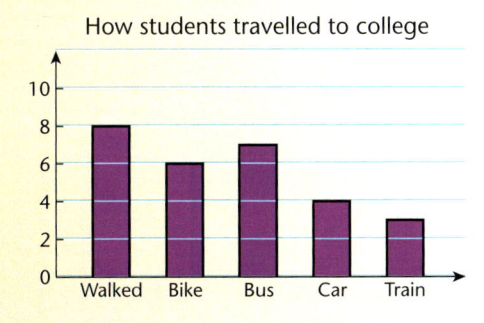

   How students travelled to college

   (Bar chart: Walked 8, Bike 6, Bus 7, Car 4, Train 3)

   One student is chosen at random from these 28 students.
   Work out the probability that they walked to college.

4 This pictograph shows the number of mobile phones stolen each term from the students in a school.

Autumn term 2004	📱
Spring term 2005	📱 📱
Summer term 2005	📱 📱 📱
Autumn term 2005	📱 📱 📱 📱
Spring term 2006	📱 📱

📱 represents 4 phones

a How many phones are represented in this pictograph?

b One of these stolen phones is chosen at random. What is the probability that it was stolen in the Summer term of 2005?

5 This table shows the times taken by 15 people to travel to work.

Time, t minutes	Frequency
$0 \leq t < 10$	3
$10 \leq t < 20$	5
$20 \leq t < 30$	7

One of these people is chosen at random.
What is the probability that their journey to work takes less than 20 minutes?

7.7 The number of times an event is likely to happen

Sometimes you need to estimate how often an event might happen.

Example 5

A game involves rolling a dice. A prize is given when a six shows. Estimate the number of prizes that will be needed for about 300 turns.

$300 \times \frac{1}{6} = 300 \div 6$
$= 50$

About 50 prizes are needed.

On one turn, the probability of winning is $\frac{1}{6}$. This means there will be about 1 win in every 6 turns. So for 300 turns there will be about $300 \times \frac{1}{6}$ wins.

**number of times that an event is likely to happen
= probability that it will happen once × number of times it is tried**

When you flip a fair coin, the probability that it will show a head is $\frac{1}{2}$.

If you flip this coin 20 times, you expect to get about 10 heads. ($\frac{1}{2} \times 20 = 10$)

What you expect to get is an *estimate*. It is not necessarily the same as what you will get.
Suppose you flip a coin 20 times and get 15 heads. This is more than the 10 heads you expect. This can happen by chance, or it could be that the coin is biased.

Exam practice 7F

1. A fair coin is flipped 100 times.
   Write down the number of heads expected.

2. A fair ordinary dice is rolled 60 times.
   Find the number of times you expect it to show 1.

3. This spinner is fair. It is spun 100 times.
   Work out the number of times you expect it to show 4.

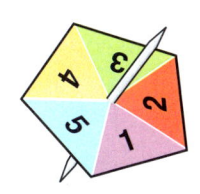

4. This spinner is fair. It is spun 40 times.
   a Find the number of times you expect it will show 1.
   b Work out the number of times you expect it will show 3.

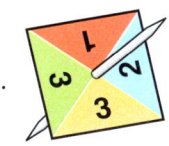

5. This fair spinner is spun 50 times.
   How often do you expect it will show an even number?

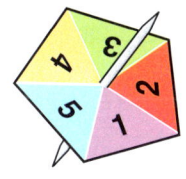

6. A ordinary fair dice is rolled 90 times.
   a Work out the number of times you expect it to show 6.
   b Work out the number of times you expect it to show an odd number.
   c Work out the number of times you expect it to show a number less than 3.

7. Middleton airport has 200 flights leaving each day.
   The probability that a plane is delayed is $\frac{1}{10}$.
   How many delayed flights are expected on one day?

8. Derek rolls two ordinary fair six-sided dice 360 times.
   The probability that they show a double six is $\frac{1}{36}$.
   Work out the number of double sixes Derek is likely to get.

9. The probability of winning a prize on a game of chance is $\frac{1}{50}$.
   500 people played the game.
   Find an estimate for the number of prizes that were won.

10 The probability that a lift will break down each time it is used is $\frac{1}{1000}$.
    The lift is used about 5000 times each year.
    Estimate the number of times that it is likely to break down.

11 Shaun goes to work by train.
    The probability that his train is late is $\frac{1}{8}$.
    Shaun works 200 days each year.
    Estimate the number of these days when Shaun's train is late.

12 a Write down the probability of getting a head on one flip of a fair coin.
    b Work out the number of heads you expect to get if you flipped the coin 60 times.
    c Angela said 'If you flip a fair coin 10 times, you will get 5 heads.'
       Is Angela correct? Give a reason for your answer.
    d Sam tossed one coin 100 times. He got 10 heads.
       Sam said 'This coin is biased.'
       Is Sam correct? Give a reason for your answer.

7.8 Games of chance

A game of chance is a game where everyone playing has the same chance of winning.

Exam practice 7G

1 Harry plays a game of chance.
   The probability of winning is $\frac{1}{10}$.
   Each go at the game costs 20p and the prize is £1.
   Harry plays this game 50 times.
   a How much does Harry spend on the game?
   b How many times is Harry likely to win?
   c How much money is Harry likely to win?
   d Is Harry likely to lose money or make money on this game?
      Give a reason for your answer.

2 The probability of winning a prize of £25 from a scratch card is $\frac{1}{50}$.
   Scratch cards cost £1 each.
   Tom buys 100 cards.
   a Work out how many times Tom is likely to win.
   b Work out how much Tom is likely to win.
   c Calculate the difference between the money Tom spends on scratch cards and his likely winnings.

3   The probability that the same symbol shows in each of the three windows on this slot machine is $\frac{1}{64}$.
    When this happens, the machine pays out £10.
    Otherwise it pays out nothing.

    a Kate plays 128 times.
       Write down the number of times that Kate is likely to win.

    b Work out the amount of money that Kate is likely to win.

    c Each turn costs 20p.
       Work out how much 128 turns costs Kate.

    d Is Kate likely to make a profit?
       Give a reason for your answer.

4   Rachael plays a game with four ordinary dice.
    The four dice are rolled.
    When at least one six shows, Rachael wins £1.
    The probability that this will happen is 0.52.
    When no sixes show Rachael loses £1.
    She plays this game 100 times.
    Is she likely to make a profit from this game?
    Give a reason for your answer.

She makes a profit if she wins more than she loses.

Summary of key points

- probability that an event happens

  $= \dfrac{\text{number of ways that the event can happen}}{\text{total number of equally likely outcomes}}$

- an estimate for the number of times an event will happen

  $=$ probability that it will happen once $\times$ the number of times it is tried

Most students who get GRADE E or above can:
- find the probability of an event when there is more than one way it can happen, for example, scoring more than 4 when a dice is rolled.

Most students who get GRADE C can also:
- give reasons why a statement may or may not be true.

Glossary

Biased	possible outcomes not equally likely
Chance	another word for probability
Equally likely	as likely an outcome as any other outcome
Event	something that happens
Experiment	something you do without knowing what will happen, for example flipping a coin
Fair	not biased
Outcome	the result of an experiment
Possible outcome	what might happen
Probability	the likelihood that something will happen expressed as a fraction or decimal between 0 and 1.
Random	chosen by chance
Unbiased	not biased

8 Probability 2

This chapter will show you:
- how to find the probability that an event does not happen
- what mutually exclusive events are
- how to use a table to give all the possible outcomes for two events
- how to use a table to find probabilities when the outcomes are equally likely
- the meaning of relative frequency and how to use it

Before you start you need to know:
- what a two-way table is
- how to work out probabilities
- how to estimate the number of times an event will happen
- how to add and subtract fractions
- how to add and subtract decimals

8.1 The probability that an event does not happen

$$\begin{pmatrix}\text{probability that an event}\\\text{will NOT happen}\end{pmatrix} = 1 - \begin{pmatrix}\text{probability that}\\\text{it will happen}\end{pmatrix}$$

You can use this fact to find the **probability** that an **event** does not happen when you know the probability that the event does happen.

For example, there are 4 ways of drawing an ace from a full pack of cards.
There are (52 − 4) ways of drawing a card that is not an ace.
The probability that an ace is NOT drawn
$= \dfrac{52-4}{52} = 1 - \dfrac{4}{52}$
$= 1 -$ probability of getting an ace.

Example 1

The probability that Joe will pass his driving test is 0.7
What is the the probability that Joe will fail his driving test?

Failing the test is the same as not passing.

The probability that Joe will fail = 1 − 0.7
= 0.3

Class discussion

1. The probability that Ann will have to wait five minutes or more for the next bus is 0.4.
What is the probability that she will have to wait less than five minutes?
2. The probability that it will rain tomorrow in Southwood is 0.3.
What is the probability that it will not rain in Southwood tomorrow?
3. A dice is biased so that the probability of scoring six is $\frac{1}{4}$.
What is the probability that when this dice is rolled it shows 1, 2, 3, 4, or 5?

Exam practice 8A

1. The probability that I will catch my bus to work tomorrow morning is 0.9.
   Calculate the probability that I will miss it.

2. Max plays tennis.
   The probability that he gets his serve in is one in ten.
   What is the probability that Max's next serve
   a goes in
   b does not go in?

3. The probability that I will score at least 65% in the next test is 0.82.
   Calculate the probability that I will score less than 65% in the next test.

4. A coin is biased. When it is flipped, the probability that it shows a head is 0.68.
   What is the probability that it shows a tail?

5. A number is chosen at random from the first 20 counting numbers.
   a Find the probability that it is a prime number.
   b Calculate the probability that it is not a prime number.

6. 500 raffle tickets are sold. Carla buys 20 tickets.
   Calculate the probability that Carla will not win first prize.

   Read this question carefully. Make sure you understand what you are asked to find.

7. Sandra needs an operation. She is told that there is a risk that the operation will not work.
   The probability that the operation will not work is $\frac{3}{100}$.
   What is the probability that the operation will work?

8. A bag contains 10p and 20p coins.
   One coin is taken out at random.
   The probability of choosing a 10p coin is 0.7.
   Find the probability of choosing a 20p coin.

   A 20p coin is not a 10p coin.

9. A pile of cards have numbers written on them. Some of the numbers are even and the rest are odd. One card is chosen at random.
   The probability that it will have an even number on it is $\frac{2}{5}$.
   Work out the probability that it will have an odd number on it.

10. This dice is biased. The probability that it gives an even number is 0.6.
    Calculate the probability that it gives an odd number.

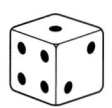

8.2 Mutually exclusive outcomes

Mutually exclusive outcomes cannot happen at the same time.

For example, when you flip a coin, it will show a head or a tail; it cannot show both.

For any experiment:

the sum of the probabilities of all the mutually exclusive outcomes is 1.

You can use this fact when you know some probabilities but not all.

When you spin this **fair** spinner, it can show 1, 2 or 3. These are mutually exclusive outcomes.

The probability that it shows 1 is

$$\frac{\text{the number of ways it can land with 1 showing (1)}}{\text{the total number of ways it can land (4)}} = \frac{1}{4}$$

The probability that it shows 2 is $\frac{1}{4}$

The probability that it shows 3 is

$$\frac{\text{the number of ways it can land with 3 showing (2)}}{\text{total number of ways it can land (4)}} = \frac{2}{4}$$

The sum of these probabilities is

$$\frac{1}{4} + \frac{1}{4} + \frac{2}{4} = \frac{4}{4} = 1$$

Example 2

A bag contains a mixture of green, yellow and blue beads. One bead is removed at random.
This table shows the probability that the bead is green and the probability that it is yellow.

Colour	Green	Yellow	Blue
Probability	0.4	0.25	

Find the probability that the bead is blue.

$$0.4 + 0.25 + (\text{probability that the bead is blue}) = 1$$
$$0.65 + (\text{probability that the bead is blue}) = 1$$
So $\quad (\text{probability that the bead is blue}) = 1 - 0.65$
$$= 0.35$$

The bead must be green or yellow or blue so these are mutually exclusive outcomes. You use the fact that the sum of the three probabilities is 1.

Exam practice 8B

1 This spinner is biased.
   The table gives the probabilities that it shows 1 or 2

Number showing	1	2	3
Probability	0.3	0.3	

Calculate the probability that it shows 3.

2. A packet contains seed for flowers that are pink, white or yellow.
The table gives the probabilities that a seed will give pink flowers or that it will give white flowers.

Colour	Yellow	White	Pink
Probability		$\frac{1}{5}$	$\frac{3}{5}$

Calculate the probability that one seed chosen at random will give yellow flowers.

3. Two biased coins are flipped.
The table shows the possible outcomes and some of the probabilities.

Outcome	2 heads	2 tails	1 head and 1 tail
Probability	$\frac{2}{9}$	$\frac{4}{9}$	

Find the probability that the coins show 1 head and 1 tail.

Biased means that they are more likely to show one side than the other.

4. Orange, blue and purple tickets are sold in a raffle.
The table shows some of the probabilities that a ticket of a particular colour will win first prize.

Ticket colour	Probability of winning first prize
Orange	0.3
Blue	
Purple	0.5

a Find the probability that a blue ticket wins the first prize.
b Which colour ticket is most likely to win?
   Explain your answer.

"Explain your answer" means write down why you chose the colour that you did.

5. The train Grace goes to work on can arrive late, early or on time.
The table gives the probabilities for each of these events.

Arrival	Late	Early	On time
Probability	0.2	0.2	

a Calculate the probability that the train will be on time.
b Grace uses this train 200 times a year.
   Estimate the number of times her train is late.

The number of times the train is expected to be late is the number of journeys × probability the train will be late.

6. A box contains a mix of 3 different varieties of eating apples.
Jane takes an apple out of the box at random.
The table shows the probabilities that the apple is one of three varieties.

Variety	Cox	Granny Smith	Golden Delicious
Probability	0.15		0.55

a Calculate the probability that Jane chooses a Granny Smith.
b There are 50 apples in the box.
   Estimate the number of Granny Smiths in the box.

7 A bag contains red, blue and green discs. One disc is drawn at random.
The probability of drawing a red disc is 0.4
The probability of drawing a green disc is 0.5.
Calculate the probability of drawing a blue disc.

> The disc drawn is either red, green or blue. These events are mutually exclusive so the sum of the their probabilities is 1.

8 A drug for migraine has different effects on different people.
The table shows the probability that the drug cures the migraine completely or reduces the pain.

Cures the migraine	Reduces the pain	Has no effect
0.4	0.4	

One person, chosen at random, tries the drug.
Work out the probability that the drug has no effect on that person.

9 Ann and Erin play a game.
The probability that Ann will win is 0.25. The probability that Ann and Erin draw is 0.5.

   a What is the probability that Ann will lose?

   b Do Ann and Erin have equal chances of winning?
Give a reason for your answer.

10 Freda places an order with an online bookshop.
The probability that her order will be one day late arriving is 0.15.
The probability that her order will be two or more days late is 0.02.
The probability that the order will not arrive is 0.01.

   a Work out the probability that the order will arrive on time.

   b Is the order more likely to be on time, late or to not arrive?
Explain your answer.

8.3 Sample spaces

A **compound event** involves more than one event.

For example, this coin is flipped and this spinner is spun.
There are two events: how the coin lands and how the spinner lands.

One possible outcome is that the coin will land head up and that the spinner will show 1. There are other possible outcomes.

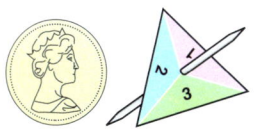

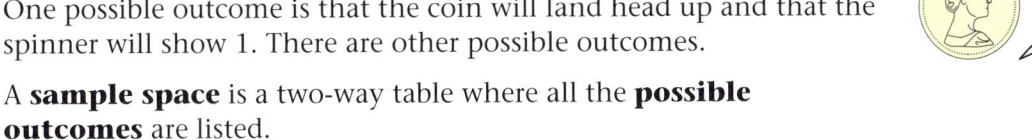

A **sample space** is a two-way table where all the **possible outcomes** are listed.

This is a sample space for the coin and the spinner.

Spinner

		1	2	3
Coin	H			
	T			

> The possible outcomes for the spinner are written across the top. The possible outcomes for the coin are written down the side.

Spinner

		1	2	3
Coin	H	H, 1	H, 2	H, 3
	T	T, 1	T, 2	T, 3

> Now you can see all the combinations that are possible. You can fill in the table using H for a head on the coin and T for a tail.

> This means a head on the coin and a 3 on the spinner.

Exam practice 8C

1. Diran plays a game with a coin and a three-sided spinner with the sections marked 2, 4 and 6.
   He tosses the coin and spins the spinner.
   Copy and complete the table to show all the possible outcomes.

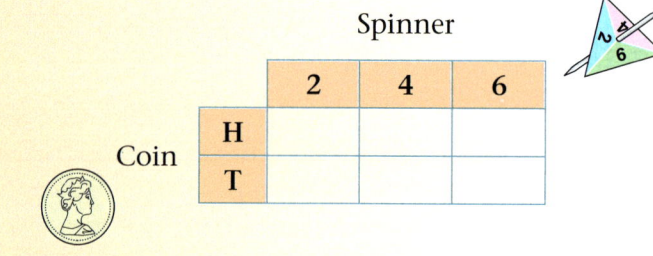

   Spinner

		2	4	6
Coin	H			
	T			

2. A six-sided dice is rolled and a coin is flipped.
   Copy and complete the table to show all the possible outcomes.

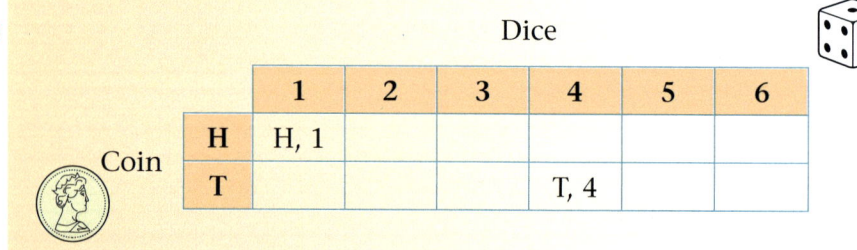

   Dice

		1	2	3	4	5	6
Coin	H	H, 1					
	T				T, 4		

3. A three-sided spinner marked 1, 2 and 3 is spun twice.
   Show all the possible outcomes in a table like this.

   1st spin

		1	2	3
2nd spin	1			
	2			
	3			

4 A disc has 1 on one side and 2 on the other.
A three-sided spinner has sections marked 1, 2 and 3.
The disc is flipped and the spinner is spun.
   a Copy and complete the table to show all the possible outcomes.

Spinner

	1	2	3
Disc 1		1, 2	
Disc 2			

   b Scott plays a game with the disc and the spinner.
He flips the coin and spins the spinner.
The scores are added together.
Copy and complete the table to show all the possible scores.

Spinner

	1	2	3
Disc 1			4
Disc 2			

5 Two spinners are spun.
One spinner is four-sided with the sections marked 1, 2, 3 and 4.
The other spinner is three-sided with the sections marked 1, 2 and 3.
The scores are added together.
Copy and complete the table to show all the possible scores.

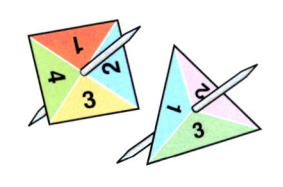

Four-sided spinner

	1	2	3	4
Three-sided spinner 1				
2				6
3				

6 Kate takes one card from the green cards and one card from the blue cards.

Green: 1 2 3
Blue: 2 4 6

The numbers on the cards are added together.
The table shows some of the possible outcomes when the numbers are added together.

Blue card

	2	4	6
Green card 1	3		
2			8
3			

   a Write down the number that goes in the grey box.
   b How many of the outcomes are the number 4?

7 Sara plays a game.
She tosses a coin and rolls a dice.
If the coin lands head up, she doubles the score on the dice.
Copy and complete the table to show all the scores that are possible.

Dice

		1	2	3	4	5	6
10p coin	H						
	T						

> Be careful: you are asked for the score, NOT the outcome. When a 1 is rolled on the dice and the coin lands head up, the score is 2.
> When a 1 is rolled and the coin shows a tail, the score is 1.

8.4 Using a sample space to find probabilities

You can count the number of outcomes from a sample space table.

Example 3

A fair coin is flipped and a fair spinner is spun.
When the coin shows a head, the score on the spinner is doubled.
When the coin shows a tail, the score on the spinner is trebled.

a Copy and complete the table.

b What is the probability of getting a score of 6?

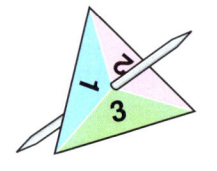

a

Spinner

		1	2	3
Coin	H	2	4	6
	T	3	6	9

> All these scores are equally likely.

b The probability that the score is 6 = $\frac{2}{6} = \frac{1}{3}$

> There are 2 sixes and 6 equally likely outcomes.

Exam practice 8D

1 Ann plays a game with two triangular spinners, one red and one green.
When they are spun, the numbers are added together to give the score.
The table shows all the possible scores.

Red spinner

		1	2	3
Green spinner	1	2	3	4
	2	3	4	5
	3	4	5	6

> Remember that probability of a score of 5
> $= \frac{\text{number of ways of scoring 5}}{\text{total number of ways of getting any score}}$

Find the probability that Ann gets a score of
a 5
b more than 3.

2 Kylie plays a game with a coin and a six-sided dice.
   She flips the coin then she rolls the dice.
   If the coin shows a head, her score on the dice is doubled.
   If the coin shows a tail, her score on the dice is the number it shows.

   The table shows all the possible scores.

		Dice					
		1	2	3	4	5	6
Coin	H	2	4	6	8	10	12
	T	1	2	3	4	5	6

   Find the probability that Kylie gets a score of
   a 2
   b less than 6.

3 This fair dice is thrown and this fair triangular spinner is spun.
   a Copy and complete the table to show all the possible outcomes.

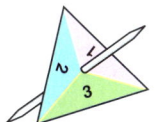

			Dice				
		1	2	3	4	5	6
	1	1, 1	1, 2				
Spinner	2	2, 1					
	3						

   b Work out the probability that the same number is scored on the dice and the spinner.

4 Amjad plays a game with the dice and the spinner in question 3.
   The score is the sum of the numbers showing on the dice and on the spinner.
   a Copy and complete the table to show all the possible scores.

			Dice				
		1	2	3	4	5	6
	1	2	3				
Spinner	2	3					
	3						

   b Work out the probability that Amjad gets a score of 5 or more.

5 One bag of coins contains three 10p coins and two 50p coins.
   Another bag contains one 10p coin and one 50p coin.
   One coin is removed at random from each bag.
   a Copy and complete the table to show all the combinations of two coins that are possible.

	1st bag				
2nd bag		10p	10p	10p	50p	50p
	10p					
	50p					

b Write down the probability that
  i both coins are 10p coins
  ii the sum of money removed is 60p.

> Read the question carefully to make sure that you understand what you are asked to find.

6 Two fair ordinary six-sided dice are rolled.
  a Copy and complete the table to show the combinations of scores that are possible.

		1st dice					
		1	2	3	4	5	6
2nd dice	1	1, 1	1, 2	1, 3			
	2	2, 1					
	3	3, 1					
	4	4, 1					
	5						
	6						6, 6

  b Write down the probability of
    i rolling a double (the same score on each dice)
    ii getting a total score of 10 or more.
  c The two dice are rolled 60 times.
    Find how many times a total score of 12 is expected.

> Draw a ring round each double in the table to help you count.

> Draw a ring round each pair of scores that add up to 10 **or** more – use a different colour to the one you used in the last part.

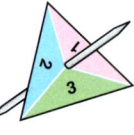

7 Summer plays a game with a fair coin and a fair three-sided spinner marked 1, 2 and 3
  She flips the coin and spins the spinner.
  When the coin shows a head, the number showing on the spinner is multiplied by 3.
  When the coin shows a tail, the number showing on the spinner is left as it is.
  a Draw a sample space table to show all the possible scores.
  b A score of 9 wins £1.
    Work out the probability of winning £1.
  c Summer decides to have 12 goes at the game.
    i How much is she likely to win?
    ii Each turn at this game costs 50p.
      Work out whether Summer is likely to make money or lose money on this game. Explain your answer.

8 Oscar flips a coin twice.
  What is the probability that he will get a head both times?

9 Lucy rolls an ordinary six-sided dice twice.
  What is the probability that she will roll a four both times?

8.5 Relative frequency

Relative frequency uses the results from an investigation to estimate the probability that an event will happen.

A dice is rolled 60 times.
Each roll of the dice is called a **trial**.

A six showed on 20 of these rolls.
The number of sixes that showed divided by the number of trials
$= \frac{20}{60} = \frac{1}{3}$.

This is the **relative frequency** of a six. You can use it to estimate the probability that a six will show next time this dice is rolled. The estimation gets better as the number of trials gets larger.

relative frequency of an event $= \dfrac{\text{number of times the event occurs}}{\text{the total number of trials}}$

Example 4

This bar chart shows the results of flipping a coin several times.

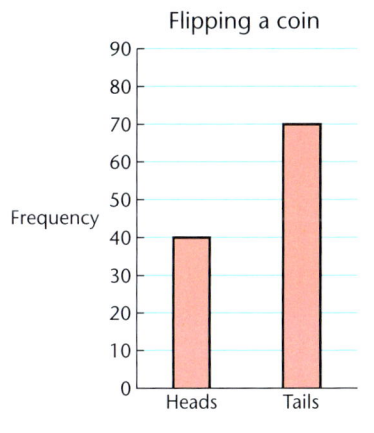

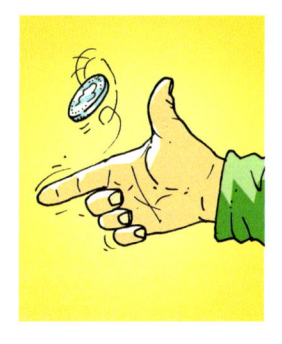

Flipping a coin (bar chart: Heads = 40, Tails = 70)

a Find the relative frequency of heads.
b Find an estimate for the probability of a head if this coin is tossed again.

a The relative frequency of heads is $\frac{40}{110}$

> There were 40 heads out of 110 flips.

b Estimate of probability of a head $= \frac{40}{110} = \frac{4}{11}$

> You use the relative frequency of a head as the estimate of probability.

> On this evidence it looks as though this coin is more likely to give a tail than a head so it may be biased.

Exam practice 8E

1. A dice is rolled.
   The scores on the first 20 rolls are

   3 5 1 4 6 2 3 5 1 4
   4 2 6 3 5 3 4 2 6 1

   a Work out the relative frequency of a 6 for these results.

   The next 10 scores are: 2 5 2 6 1 4 6 3 4 5

   b Calculate the relative frequency of a 6 after all 30 rolls.
   c Write down an estimate of the probability that this dice shows a six when rolled.
   d Do you think this dice is unbiased? Give a reason for your answer.

   > Count the number of 6s and express this as a fraction of the total number of scores.

2. A dice is numbered 1 to 6 but it is biased.
   The scores from 20 rolls of this dice are given in the table.

Roll number	1	2	3	4	5	6	7	8	9	10
Score	3	1	5	6	2	4	6	4	5	5

Roll number	11	12	13	14	15	16	17	18	19	20
Score	6	2	6	3	1	2	1	6	4	6

   a Use the first ten scores to estimate the probability that the score will be 6.
   b Use just the next ten scores to estimate the probability that the score will be 6.
   c Use all the scores to estimate the probability that the score will be 6.
   d It is claimed that the probability of scoring a 6 with this dice is 0.29.
      Do these results support this claim? Give a reason for your answer.

3. A coin was flipped 100 times. The coin showed a head 70 times.
   a Estimate the probability that this coin will show a head.
   b Estimate the number of heads you would expect if this coin is flipped 10 times.

4. A survey into voting intentions found that 50 of the 120 adults questioned said they would not vote in the local elections.
   a Estimate the probability that an adult chosen at random says they will not vote.
   b There are 25 000 people on the electoral register.
      Work out an estimate for the number of people who will vote.

5. Clara makes up a game of chance. She plays the game fifty times and wins twice.
   a Estimate the probability that anyone who plays the game will win.
   b Clara estimates that about 200 people will play the game.
      Anyone who wins will be given a prize.
      Work out an estimate for the number of prizes that will be won.

6 Packs of balloons contain red, blue and white balloons.
Jon counted the number of each colour in several packs.
The table gives the results.

Colour	Red	Blue	White
Frequency	125	143	132

   a One balloon is chosen at random from a pack.
   Estimate the probability that it is white.
   b A pack contains 100 balloons.
   Find an estimate for the number of white balloons in the pack.

7 This table shows a sample of Year 10 students with and without jobs.

Students in Year 10

	Job	No job
Boys	32	19
Girls	28	21

   a A girl is chosen at random from this sample.
   Find the probability that she has a job as a fraction in its lowest terms.
   b A student is chosen at random from all Year 10 students.
   Estimate the probability that the student does not have a job.

Student means boy or girl.

8 The table shows last year's Key Stage 3 results for Year 9.

King School – Key Stage 3 levels

	3	4	5	6	7
Boys	8	12	28	25	21
Girls	10	12	30	27	27

   a Calculate the number of boys.
   b A Year 9 student at this school is chosen at random.
   Find the probability that this student had reached level 7.
   c In one town there were 5000 students who sat Key Stage 3 tests last year.
   Estimate how many of them got level 6 or 7.

You need to find the sum of all the numbers in the 'boys' row.

9 There are 200 sweets in this bag.
Wayne took one sweet out of the bag at random, wrote down its colour, and then put it back in the bag.
He did this 200 times.
The table shows how many colours Wayne found and how many times he took that colour out of the bag.

Red	30
Green	50
Yellow	88
Orange	32

   a Fran said 'There are 50 green sweets in the bag.'
   Is she correct? Give a reason for your answer.
   b If Wayne takes another sweet out of the bag, estimate the probability that it will not be green.

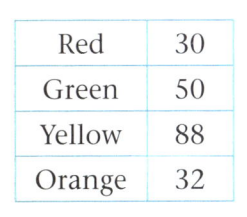

Mini coursework task

If you throw a fair dice 60 times, then you would expect to get each score 10 times. A frequency table would look like this.

Score	1	2	3	4	5	6
Frequency	10	10	10	10	10	10

a Find the mean score of this theoretical distribution.

If you throw a dice 60 times, you will be very unlikely to get equal numbers of each score. But, if your dice is unbiased, and if you throw it fairly, you should get a mean score near to the theoretical mean.

b Throw a dice 60 times, record your results and find your mean score.
How does your mean compare with the theoretical mean?
Can you say whether your dice is likely to be unbiased?
You must explain your answer.

Summary of key points

- (probability that an event does NOT happen)
  = 1 − (the probability that it does happen)
- The sum of the probabilities of all mutually exclusive outcomes is 1.
- A compound event involves more than one event. Tossing two coins is a compound event.
- You can use a two-way table to list all the possible outcomes for two events.
- When all the outcomes of two events are equally likely, you can use the two-way table to find the probability that a particular outcome will happen.
- Relative frequency is calculated from frequencies of events that have already happened and can be used to estimate the probability that an event will occur next time the experiment is repeated.

Most students who get Grade E or above can:
- use a two-way table to work out probabilities.

Most students who get grade C can also:
- understand and use relative frequency.

Glossary

Biased	possible outcomes not equally likely
Compound events	more than one event
Equally likely outcomes	each outcome is as likely to happen as any other outcome
Event	thing that happens
Fair	not biased
Mutually exclusive	cannot both happen
Possible outcome	what might happen
Probability	the likelihood that something will happen expressed as a fraction or a decimal between 0 and 1.
Random	chosen by chance
Relative frequency	the number of times a particular event has occurred divided by the total number of trials
Sample space	a table showing all possible outcomes
Trial	a single observation or experiment such as a roll of a dice or a flip of a coin
Unbiased	not biased, fair

9 Conclusions

This chapter will show you:
- ✓ what conclusions you can and cannot draw from statistics
- ✓ how to compare two sets of statistics
- ✓ how assumptions can affect results

Before you start you need to know:
- ✓ the meaning of mean, mode, median and range
- ✓ the meaning of a survey and a sample
- ✓ how to get information from a frequency table and a two-way table
- ✓ how to find a fraction of a quantity
- ✓ how to get information from bar charts, frequency polygons, pie charts and stem-and-leaf diagrams

9.1 Drawing conclusions

When you do a **survey**, your results are true only for the **data** collected.
The results can only be used as an *estimate* for the whole population.

People can distrust statistics because survey results are often taken to be true for the whole population.

Did you know
that a British Prime Minister, called Disraeli, said 'There are lies, dammed lies and statistics'?
This is still quoted today.
This chapter will help you understand why people believe this.

Example 1

An opinion poll was based on a sample of 500 people. Give a reason why this headline may not be accurate.

It assumes that the opinion of 500 people is the same as all adults but does not say so. It is only an estimate for the opinions of all adults.

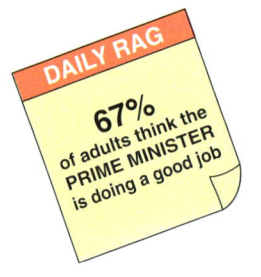

DAILY RAG
67% of adults think the PRIME MINISTER is doing a good job

An estimate may or may not be nearly accurate. It depends on how the **sample** was chosen and the size of the sample.

Another reason that people can distrust statistics is that statements that are true do not tell the whole story. You need to look at the data to decide if conclusions are only partly true.

Using the word average can cause misunderstanding. You do not know if it is the **median**, the **mean** or the **mode**.

You will see this warning on packets of cigarettes: 'Smoking Kills'
The statement comes from statistical research that shows that smoking kills more than 50% of smokers.
'Smoking Kills' is true but does not give all the information.

Example 2

Ten students took a test.
These are the marks: 5, 5, 5, 5, 5, 6, 6, 6, 10, 10
Tariq said 'Half the students got more than the average mark.'
Is Tariq right?

The mode is 5

The median mark is 5.5

The mean mark is $\dfrac{5+5+5+5+5+6+6+6+10+10}{10} = \dfrac{63}{10} = 6.3$

Tariq is right if he is using the median but wrong if he is using the mean.

There are three averages. You need to find each of them.

Assumptions are often made that can affect the result of a survey.
This often happens with questions on a questionnaire.

Example 3

A sample of people were asked this question.
'If there was a general election tomorrow, which party would you vote for?'
52% said they would vote for Party A.
Sophie said 'That means Party A will get 52% of the vote.'
Give one assumption that Sophie has made.

Sophie has assumed that all the people who said they would vote for Party A will actually vote.

Class discussion

1 A coin was flipped five times. The coin showed a head 4 times and a tail once. David said 'This coin is more likely to give a head than a tail.' What assumption had David made?
2 The mean height of children in year 7 is 1.4 m. Emily said 'that means that half the children in year 7 are taller than 1.4 m.' What assumption has Emily made?

Exam practice 9A

1 This is a report from a newspaper:
'80% of people in the UK are against the selection of a baby's gender for social reasons.'
This conclusion comes from the views of a sample of people.
Explain why the figure of 80% is not exact.

Read each question carefully. Make sure that you know what you are asked to find.

2 A politician promised this: 'If I am elected, I will make sure that everyone earns more than the average salary.'
Give one reason why he cannot do this.

3 A report on a television news programme said that the average pocket money received by ten-year-olds is £4.00 a week.
Greg said 'That means that half of ten-year-olds get less than £4.00 a week.'
Is Greg correct? Justify your answer.

4 A survey into the number of bedrooms in new houses was carried out.
This frequency polygon shows the distribution of the number of bedrooms.
   a How many houses have 4 bedrooms?
   b Jake said 'Three bedrooms is the average.'
Which two averages could Jake be using? Explain your answer.

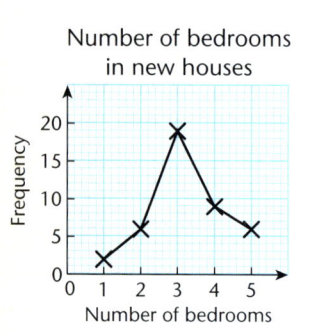

5 Tom grows tomatoes in a greenhouse. He chose a sample of his tomatoes and weighed each of these tomatoes.
The **frequency table** shows the results.

Weight, w grams	$10 \leq w < 15$	$15 \leq w < 20$	$20 \leq w < 25$	$25 \leq w < 30$
Frequency	5	16	12	7

   a Write down the number of tomatoes in the sample.
   b One of these tomatoes is chosen at random.
      What is the probability that it weighs less than 15 grams?
   c Tom expects to harvest 8000 tomatoes.
      Estimate how many will weigh less than 15 grams.
      Explain why your answer is an estimate and not exact.

6 Gina did a survey on pay for part-time work. She asked a sample of 20 part-time workers how much they were paid an hour.
The stem-and-leaf diagram shows her results.

Part time hourly pay   5|00 means £5.00

```
5 | 00  00  10  10  20  30  50  50  50  90
6 | 00  00  20  50  50  80
7 | 50
8 | 00  00  90
```

Gina said that most part-time workers in her survey earn less than £6.00 an hour.
Is she correct?
Give a reason for your answer.

7 These are the salaries paid to the people working in a restaurant.
£6000, £6000, £10 000, £10 000, £10 000, £15 000, £20 000, £40 000

   a Write down the median salary.
   b Write down the mode.
   c Work out the mean salary.
   d Jude asked 'What is the average salary?'
   Write down what you would tell Jude.
   Explain your answer.

8 A sample of 100 people were asked if they owned a car.
The table shows the results.

	Men	Women
Own a car	50	35
Do not own a car	5	10

   a Work out the **proportion** of the sample who are women and do not own a car.
   b The survey was carried out in a town with a population of 20 000.
   Estimate the number of women in the town who do not own a car.
   c Explain why your answer to part **b** can only be an estimate.

> This means you have to find the number of women who do not own a car. Then you put this number over the total number of people in the sample. Simplify the fraction.

9 The table shows some Year 10 students with and without jobs.
   a What proportion of the students did not have a job?
   b There are 3000 students in Year 10 at schools in the county.
   Can you work out exactly how many of these students did not have a job?
   Explain your answer.

Students in Year 10

	Job	No job
Boys	32	22
Girls	28	18

10 The **time-series graph** shows the average yearly rate of inflation month by month for the first eight months of the year.
Gordon looked at this graph and said 'The rate of inflation will be below 2% by the end of the year.'
Write down one assumption that Gordon has made.

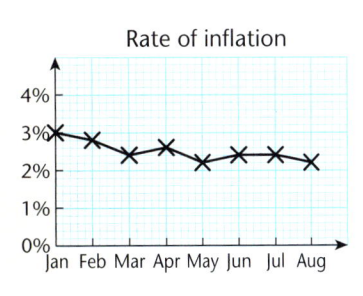

11 The **scatter graph** shows the number of pets and the number of children in a sample of households.
Owen drew a **line of best fit**.
He said 'A household with a lot of children has several pets.'
Is Owen correct that the graph shows this relationship?
Justify your answer.

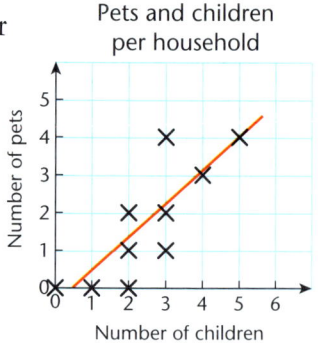

12 A sample of people were asked how many books they read a month.
They were also asked their heights.
The scatter graph shows the results.
Jane said 'This graph shows that there is a strong relationship between your height and the number of books you read. This means that reading more books will make you taller.'
Is Jane correct?
Explain your answer.

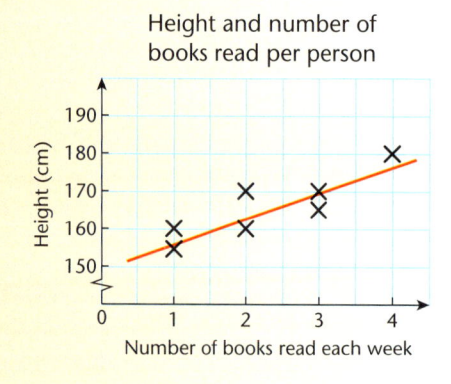

9.2 Comparing data

When you compare two sets of data, use only the facts you know.

Example 4

Thirty students sat a maths exam. The mean mark was 56%.
Six months later, the same students sat another maths exam.
This time the mean mark was 75%.
Give one difference between the two sets of marks.

> The mean mark for the first exam is lower than the mean mark for the second exam.

Do not try to give reasons why the means are different. These are assumptions.
You cannot say
- the first exam was harder than the second exam
- the students had improved at maths when they sat the second exam.

Dual charts

Two sets of information are often put on the same diagram.
This makes it easier to compare the data.

Example 5

This **bar chart** shows the number of students getting each grade in French and in history.
Give three differences between the grades for French and history.

A* to E grades in French and history at Purslow School

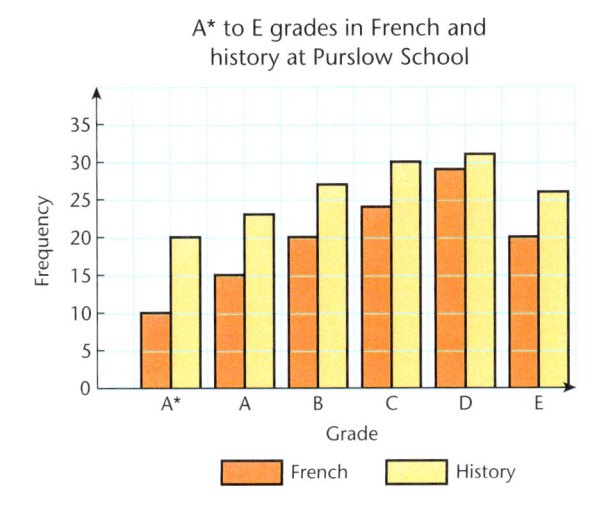

There were 10 A* grades in French and 20 A* grades in history.
There were more passes at every grade in history than in French.
The difference between the numbers getting a particular grade is greatest for grade A*.

> You do not know *why* there were more passes at every grade in history than in French. So you cannot say that the students who did history were cleverer than the students who did French.

Exam practice 9B

1. These two **pie charts** compare the age profiles of two regions of a country.

    Age profile

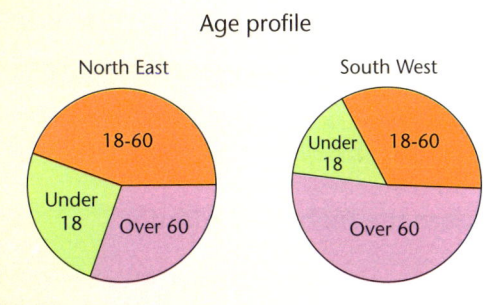

    North East / South West

    a. Which area has the larger proportion of people over 60 years old?
    b. Ashad said 'The fraction of people under 18 in the South West is about half that of the North East.'
       Is Ashad correct? Give a reason for your answer.

2 These pie charts show how two local authorities divide their spending.

Describe two differences between the local authorities.

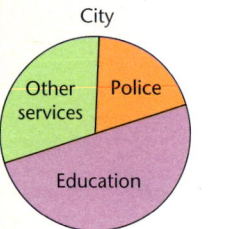

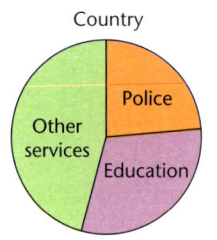

Local authority expenditure

City — Other services, Police, Education

Country — Other services, Police, Education

3 The bar chart shows the three-monthly rainfall in New York and Sydney.
  a Write down the name of the place that has the most rainfall in the first half of the year.
  b Write down the rainfall in New York from April to June.
  c Kieran said that the rainfall in Sydney was always more than in New York.
  Is Kieran correct?
  Give a reason for your answer.

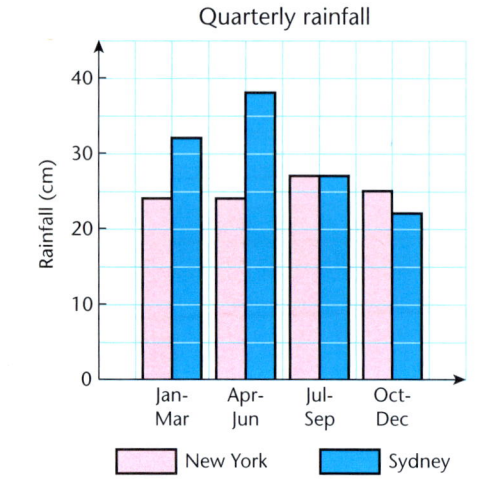

Quarterly rainfall

4 The bar chart shows the minimum and maximum temperature in London for three-monthly periods.

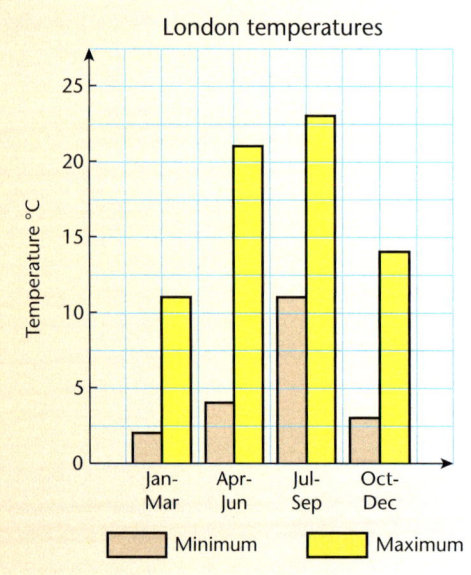

London temperatures

  a In which three-monthly period does the highest maximum temperature occur?
  b In which three-monthly period does the lowest maximum temperature occur?
  c Write down the minimum temperature from July to September.
  d Write down the period over which the difference between the maximum and minimum temperature is greatest.

5 The bar chart shows the number of absences in a class during a 'flu' epidemic.
   a Write down the number absent on Thursday of the first week.
   b Write down the number absent on Tuesday of the second week.
   c How many more were absent on the Wednesday of the second week than the Wednesday of the first week?
   d Write down one difference between the number of absences for the two weeks.

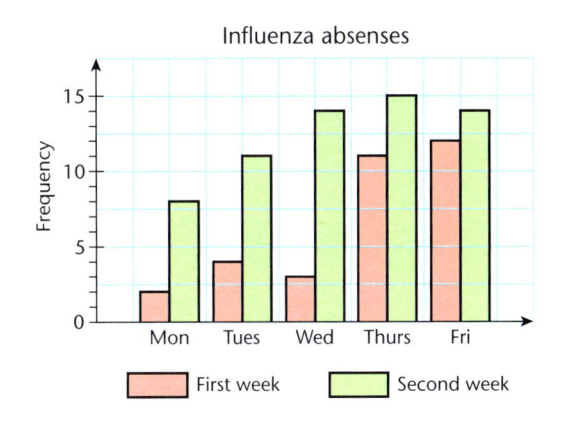

6 This chart shows the structure of a population, by age, in 1995 and 2005.

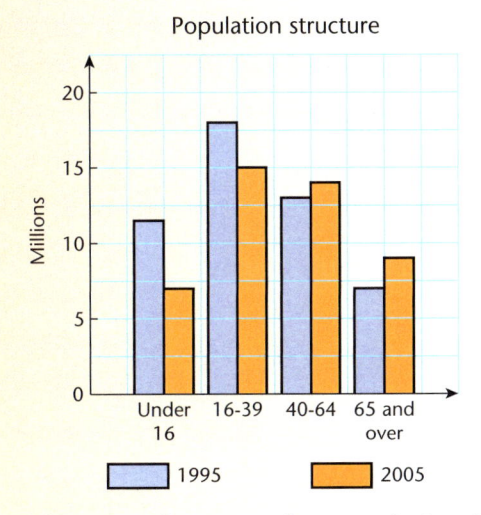

   Describe two differences between the population in 1995 and 2005.

   > Look at total population, modal age groups, sizes of the groups. You do not need to work out the mean or the median.

7 The bar chart shows the average daily sunshine in St Andrews and Sandown.

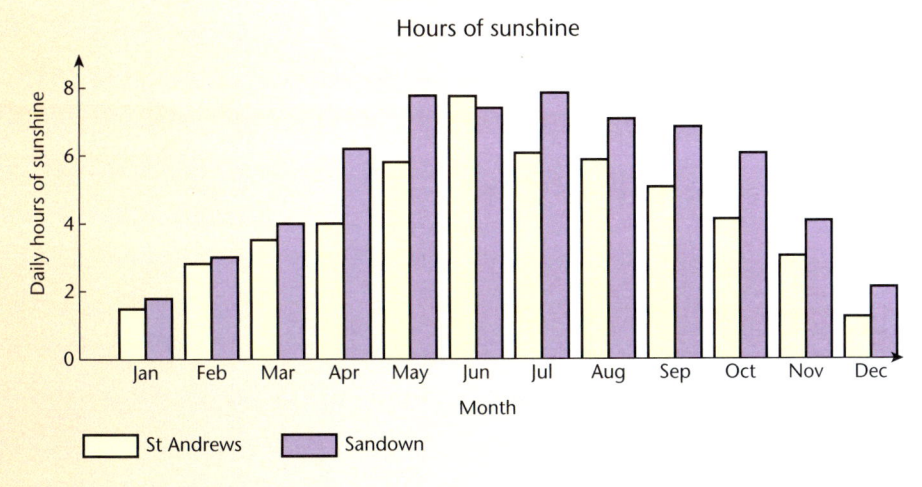

   Describe two differences between the distributions.

8 The bar chart shows the distribution of exam grades for English.
The table shows the distribution of exam grades for the same students in mathematics.

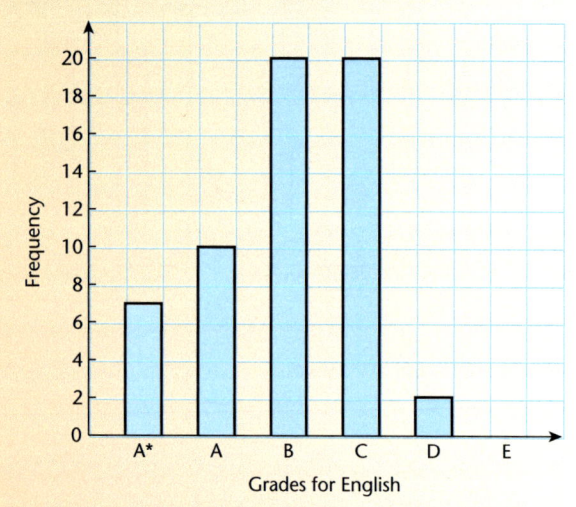

Grades for maths

Grades	Frequency
A*	4
A	6
B	15
C	18
D	11
E	5

Grades for English

Describe two differences between the distributions.

9 The stem-and-leaf diagram shows the distribution of the times taken to complete an assault course.

Times taken to complete an assault course

```
       Females                    Males
                  45 | 3 | 40  45  55
            50 18 10 | 4 | 10  12  20  45
      20 16 15 10 00 | 5 | 05  08
```

3|40 means 3 minutes 40 seconds

a Work out the range of times for the males.
b Work out the range of times for the females.
c Write down two differences between the times for the males and the times for the females.

10 Anne counted the number of words in each sentence on the front page of a newspaper.
She also counted the number of words in each sentence in the first paragraph of a book.
The stem-and-leaf diagram shows her results.

Number of words per sentence

```
        Book                Newspaper
            8 6 | 0 | 4  4  5  5  7
          9 5 3 | 1 | 0  0  1  3  7
        9 6 5 0 | 2 | 1  5  9
```

1|4 means 14 words

a Work out the median for the newspaper.
b Work out the median for the book.

c Write down one difference between these two sets of data.
d Anne wrote 'The data shows that the sentences in books are longer than the sentences in newspapers.'
Is she correct? Justify your answer.

11 Sasha asked a sample of people to estimate the length of the line A and the length of the line B.

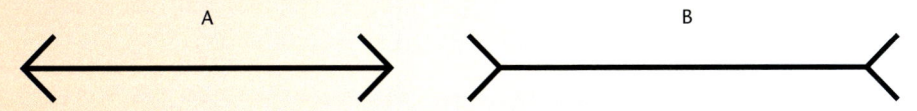

The dual frequency polygon shows her results.

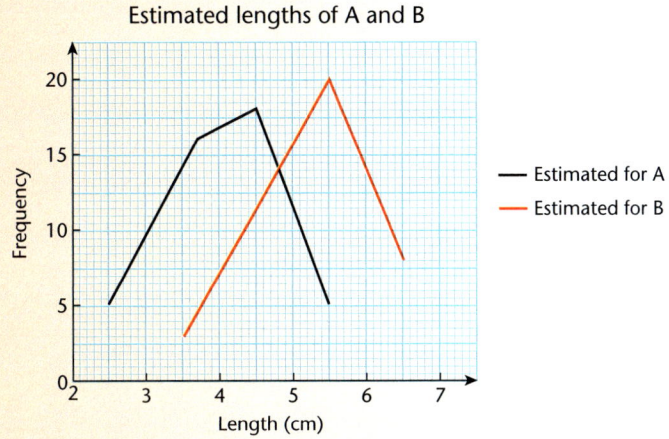

Describe two differences between the estimates for line A and the estimates for line B.

12 The frequency distribution shows marks in a science test.

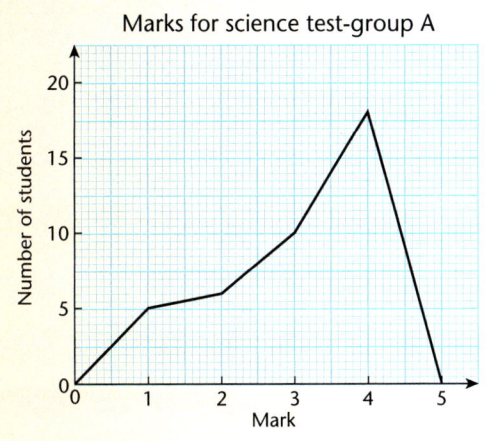

The frequency table shows the marks in the same test but for a different group of students.

Marks for science test – group B

Mark	0	1	2	3	4	5
Frequency	4	8	12	15	5	3

a On a copy of the diagram above, draw a frequency polygon to show these marks.
b Describe two differences between the marks of the two groups of students.

13 This bar chart shows the number of defective radios produced by two production lines.

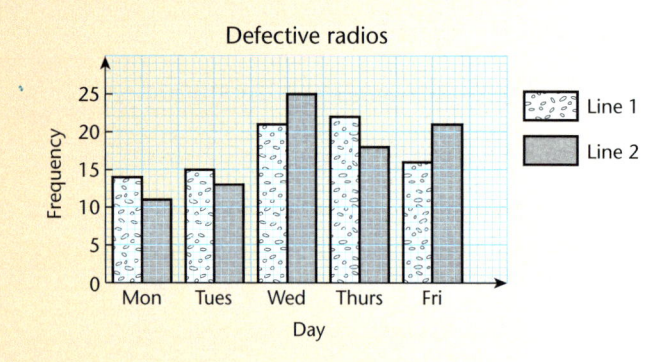

Defective radios

a Write down the line that had made the larger number of defective radios on Thursday.
b Which line made the smaller number of defective radios on Tuesday?
c Find the total number of defective radios made on Wednesday.
d Describe one difference between the two production lines.

Summary of key points

- When you make conclusions about data, everything you write must be based on facts. You must not write anything that you cannot base on facts.
- When you compare sets of data, use only facts that you know.

Most students who get GRADE E or above can:
- compare the mean, mode and range of two sets of data.

Most students who get GRADE C can also:
- use the mean, the range and the group containing the median to compare two sets of grouped data.

Glossary

Bar chart	a diagram with bars of equal width whose heights give frequencies
Data	factual information
Frequency polygon	a line graph formed by plotting frequencies against values, or mid-interval values for grouped data.
Frequency table	a table listing all the possible values, or groups of values, and their frequencies
Hypothesis	a statement that may or may not be true
Line of best fit	a line drawn through points on a scatter graph so that the points are evenly distributed about the line
Median	the middle value when a set of values is in order
Mean	the sum of the values divided by the number of values
Mode	the most popular value
Pie chart	a circle divided into slices whose sizes represent the fraction that each group is of the whole
Proportion	the fraction that one quantity is of another
Sample	some, but not all, of the items being investigated
Scatter graph	a diagram of points representing two sets of information
Stem-and-leaf diagram	a way of arranging data in groups without losing individual values
Survey	investigation based on a sample
Time-series graph	a graph showing how values change over time

Examination practice paper

Section A Time allowed : 25 minutes Calculator allowed

1 The bar chart shows the different hair colours of Year 11 pupils.

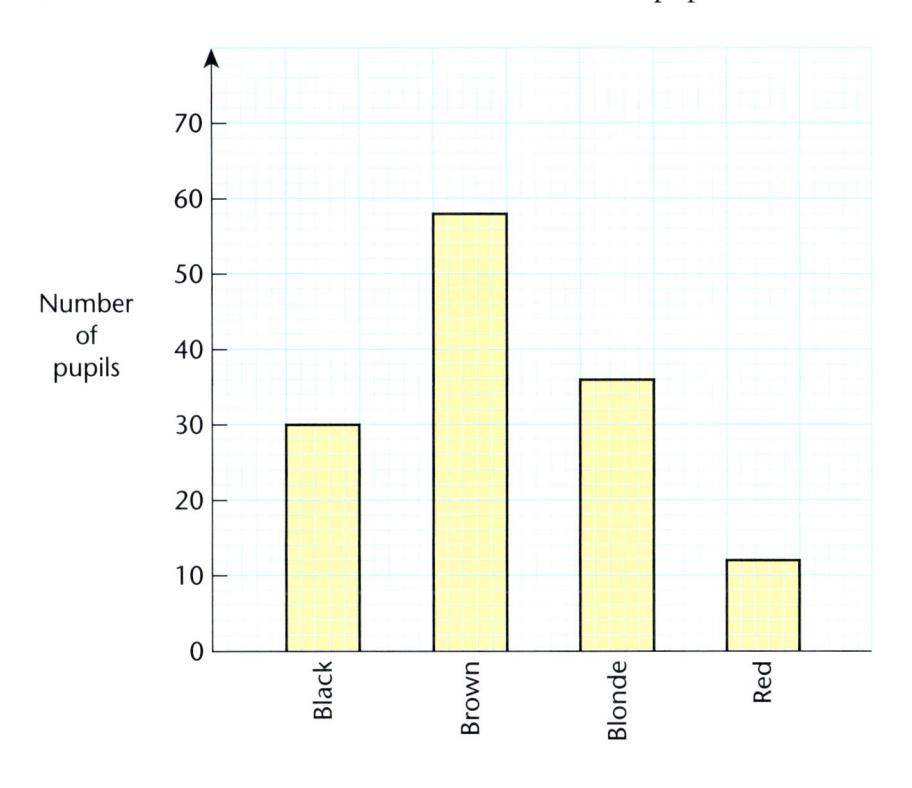

(a) Which is the hair colour that belongs to the smallest number of Year 11 pupils?
(1 mark)

(b) How many Year 11 pupils have brown hair? *(1 mark)*

(c) How many more Year 11 pupils have blonde hair than have black hair? *(1 mark)*

(d) How many Year 11 pupils are there altogether? *(2 marks)*

2 (a) Here are three events.

   Event A   Rolling the number 2 on an ordinary six-sided dice

   Event B   Winning a raffle when you have bought 1 ticket and 1000 tickets have been sold

   Event C   A fair coin lands on tails

   Write the events in order of how likely they are to happen. Start with the most likely event. *(2 marks)*

(b) There are three flavours of sweet in a bag. The flavours are orange, lemon and lime. The probability of picking a flavour is shown in the table.

Flavour of sweet	orange	lemon	lime
Probability	0.7	0.2	0.2

   (i) Explain how you know that there is a mistake in the table. *(1 mark)*

   (ii) Kim and Alex are sharing the sweets. Kim has first pick and takes all of the lemon sweets.
   What is the probability that Alex will get a lemon sweet in her share? *(1 mark)*

3 (a) Pupils at a school were asked how they travelled to school. The results are shown in the pie chart.

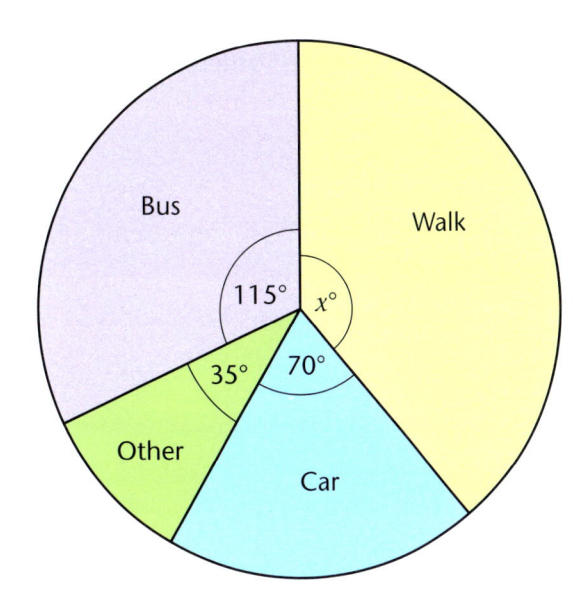

(i) Show that angle *x* is 140°. *(1 mark)*

(ii) 210 pupils came to school by car.
How many pupils walked to school? *(2 marks)*

(b) This pie chart shows the way that 90 teachers came to school.

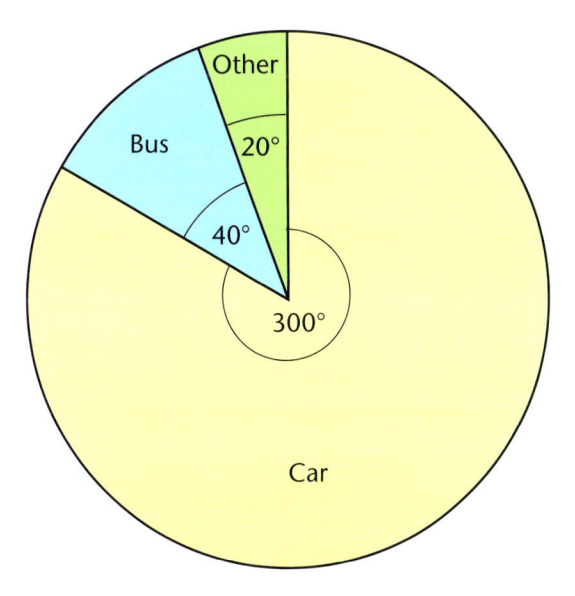

How many teachers came to school by bus? *(2 marks)*

4 Joe has the following examination marks.

56   42   77   46   65   42   59   70   61   49

(a) The marks are to be converted into an ordered stem-and-leaf diagram.

The table below has been started.
Complete the table.

Key   5 | 6   represents   56

```
4 | 2
5 | 6
6 |
7 |
```

(2 marks)

(b) Work out the range of his marks. *(1 mark)*

5 The times that 50 shoppers had to wait at a supermarket checkout one Saturday morning are shown.

Number of minutes, t	Frequency	Midpoint
$0 < t \leq 4$	10	
$4 < t \leq 8$	20	
$8 < t \leq 12$	12	
$12 < t \leq 16$	8	

Complete the midpoint column and use it to calculate an estimate of the mean number of minutes that the shoppers had to wait. *(3 marks)*

Section B

Time allowed : 25 minutes   Calculator are not allowed

1 The favourite pet of 20 people is shown.

dog	hamster	cat	hamster	dog	dog	dog	cat
cat	cat	dog	rabbit	dog	hamster	dog	cat
dog	hamster	cat	rabbit				

(a) Complete the tally and frequency columns in the table below.

Type of pet	Tally	Frequency
Dog		
Hamster		
Cat		
Rabbit		

(2 marks)

(b) Draw a pictogram to show these results.

Use the symbol ◯ to represent 4 pets.

Dog	
Hamster	
Cat	
Rabbit	

(2 marks)

(c) Sort the pets into order of popularity starting with the least popular.   *(2 marks)*

2 The graph shows the number of people watching a play during a week.

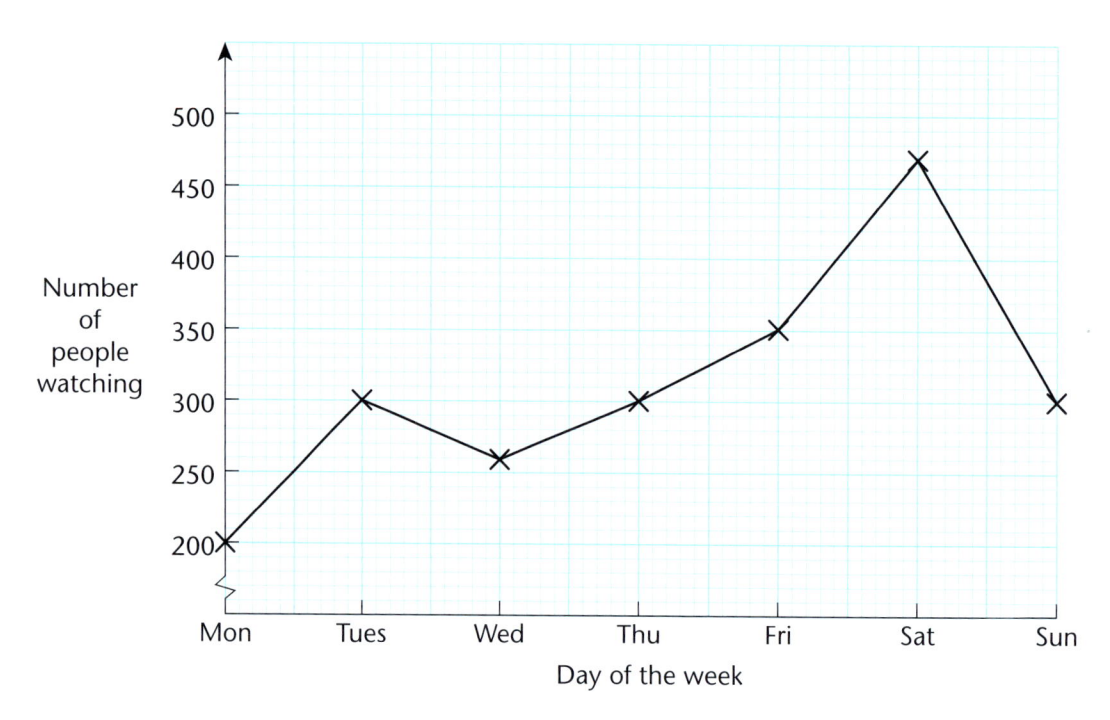

(a) On which day were there 260 people watching the play? *(1 mark)*

(b) What was the modal number of people watching the play? *(1 mark)*

(c) Work out the mean number of people watching the play during the weekend (Saturday and Sunday). *(2 marks)*

3 Here are two spinners.

Spinner A has the numbers 1, 3 and 5   Spinner B has the numbers 2, 4 and 6

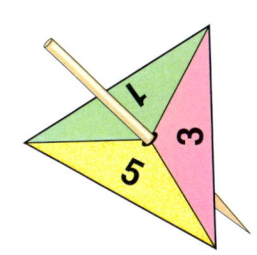

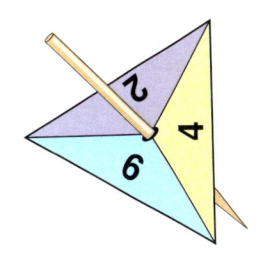

Tony spins both spinners and adds together the two numbers.

(a) Complete the table to show all the totals that Tony can get.

		Spinner A		
		1	3	5
Spinner B	2			
	4			
	6			

(2 marks)

(b) Work out the probability that Tony gets

    (i) a total that is an odd number *(1 mark)*

    (ii) a total that is 7 or less. *(2 marks)*

4 (a) A cafe sells hot drinks. The table shows the number of hot drinks it sells and the average temperature during one week.

Number of hot drinks sold	46	37	38	35	40	52	44
Temperature (°C)	20	25	23	26	22	19	21

    (i) Plot the data as a scatter graph on a grid below like the one on the next page.

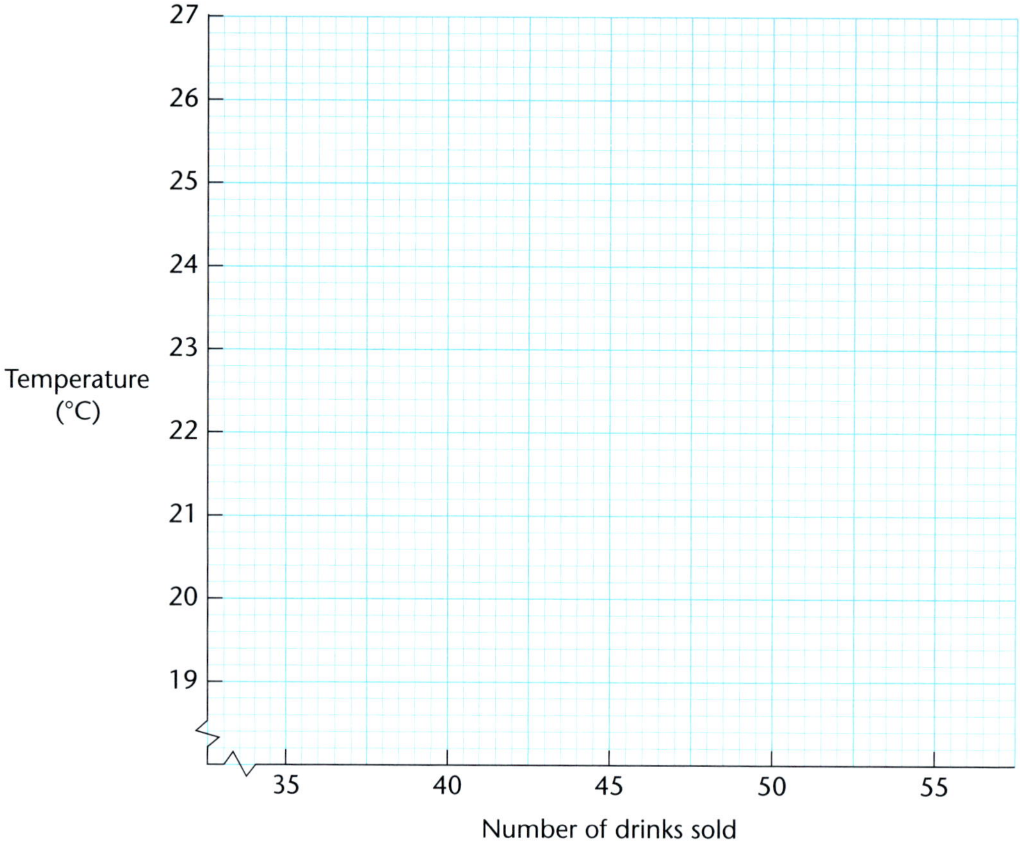

(2 marks)

(ii) Draw a line of best fit on the scatter graph. *(1 mark)*

(iii) Use your line of best fit to estimate the temperature when the shop sells 42 hot drinks. *(1 mark)*

(iv) State the type of correlation shown by the graph. *(1 mark)*

(b) Here is a scatter graph for which there is no line of best fit.

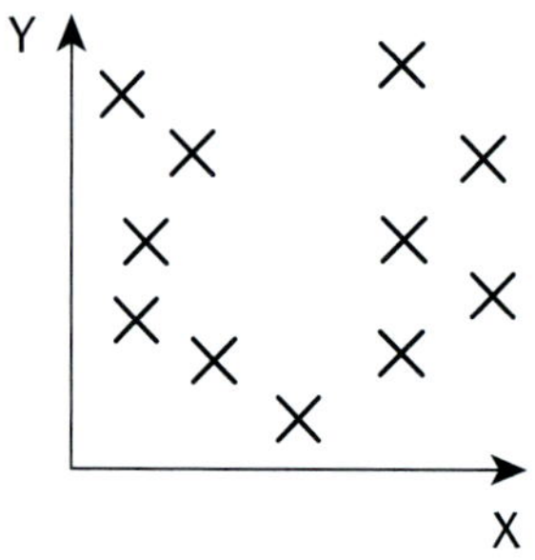

Complete this sentence by writing in the missing word.

There is no .... correlation between X and Y. *(1 mark)*

Answers

Exam practice 1A

1. 'Fat' or 'young' do not have an exact meaning.
2. a 'Fit' or 'ill' or 'very often' do not have an exact meaning.
   b 'Young' or 'interest in politics' do not have an exact meaning.
   c 'Young' or 'old' or 'more' do not have exact meanings.
3. a 'Increasing the price of all alcohol by 50% will result in fewer people being convicted for being drunk.'
   b You cannot increase the price of alcohol so you cannot test this.

Exam practice 1B

These answers are 'for example'. There is no one correct answer. Any justifiable reason is correct.
1. a Secondary data (e.g. sports day records)
   b Secondary data (e.g. weather records)
   c Secondary data (e.g. car brochures)
   d Primary data (ask students in your class which they prefer)
2. a Reaction times of boys and girls
   b Ask some boys and some girls to do a task involving reactions and time them (e.g. computer driving games)

Exam practice 1C

1. A survey. It is one school out of many.
2. A survey. She cannot do all possible rolls of this dice.
3. It could take too long and is too broad a subject.
4. It could take too long and cost too much
5. It is survey. He cannot ask everyone who might shop in either place.

Exam practice 2A

1. a qualitative
   b quantitative
   c quantitative
2. a quantitative
   b qualitative
   c quantitative
3. a quantitative
   b quantitative
   c quantitative
   d qualitative

Exam practice 2B

1. a 9   b 5, 9, 7, 21   c 21
2. a 10   b 10, 14, 7, 3, 34   c 34
3. a 19   b 19, 13, 17, 49   c 6
4. a 8, 11, 9, 8, 2, 38   b 8   c 38

Exam practice 2C

1. a & b

Colour	Tally	Frequency
yellow	卌 卌 ll	12
green	卌 卌 l	11
pink	卌 卌 lll	13
	Total	36

   c pink

2.

Shoe size	Tally	Frequency
29	卌 ll	7
30	卌 卌 l	11
31	卌 卌	10
32	卌	5
	Total	33

3.

Number of children	Tally	Frequency
0		
1		
2		
3		
4		
5+		

4. a 80   b 240
5. a 62   b 4

Exam practice 2D

1. a 22, 28, 24   b 74   c 24
2. a 17, 11, 8, 2   b 17   c 10
3. a 17, 22, 28, 16, 20, 103   b 36
   c 39   d 103
   e 25 is in the middle of a group so we do not know how many of the marks are 21 to 24
4. a 20   b 60
   c Don't know how many in the group 41–60 are below 50.

Answers

5

Mark	Tally	Frequency
1–10	ⅢⅠ	5
11–20	ⅢⅠ ⅢⅠ ⅠⅠⅠ	13
21–30	ⅢⅠ ⅢⅠ	10
	Total	28

6 a & b

Number of words	Tally	Frequency
1–5	ⅢⅠ ⅢⅠ ⅢⅠ ⅢⅠ ⅠⅠⅠⅠ	24
6–10	ⅢⅠ ⅢⅠ ⅠⅠⅠ	13
11–15	ⅠⅠ	2
	Total	39

7 e.g.

Number of seats	Tally	Frequency
1–10		
11–20		
21–30		
31–40		
41–50		
	Total	

Exam practice 2E

1 a 7, 12, 9, 2   b 19
2 a 19   b 8
   c $24 \leq h < 27$ d 51

3

Time, t sec	Tally	Frequency
$5 \leq t < 10$		
$10 \leq t < 15$		
$15 \leq t < 20$		
$20 \leq t < 25$		
	Total	

4 a & b 10, 11, 14, 11   c 46
5 a $5 \leq t < 10$ b 4   c 6
6 a 121   b $80 \leq k < 100$
   c 202   d i 192   ii $\frac{96}{101}$

Exam practice 2F

1

	can swim	can't swim
men		
women		

2

	direct dial	broadband
business		
home users		

3 Number of bedrooms

	0	1	2	3	4+
0					
1					
2					
3+					

Number of bathrooms (row label)

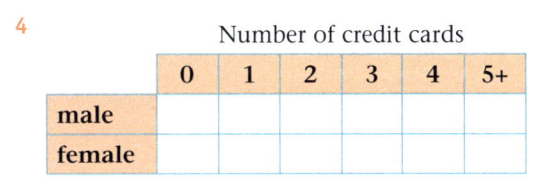

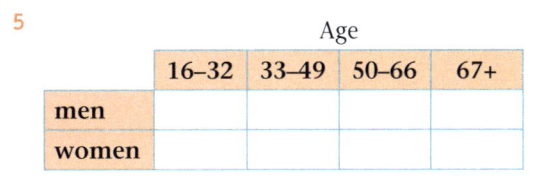

4 Number of credit cards

	0	1	2	3	4	5+
male						
female						

5 Age

	16–32	33–49	50–66	67+
men				
women				

6 Height h cm

	$90 \leq h < 100$	$100 \leq h < 110$	$100 \leq h < 120$	$120 \leq h$
$20 \leq w < 25$				
$25 \leq w < 30$				
$30 \leq w < 35$				

Weights w kg (row label)

7 Colour

	white	pink	red
$20 \leq h < 30$			
$30 \leq h < 40$			
$40 \leq h < 50$			
$50 \leq h < 60$			

Heights of plants h cm (row label)

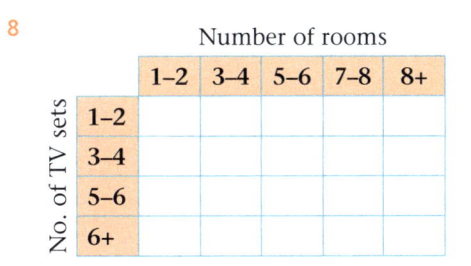

8 Number of rooms

	1–2	3–4	5–6	7–8	8+
1–2					
3–4					
5–6					
6+					

No. of TV sets (row label)

Exam practice 2G

These answers are 'for example'. There is no one correct answer. Any justifiable reason is correct.

1 It can't reach people with full-time jobs.
2 The survey concentrates on a particular group - car users.
3 A road outside a school is not a typical road in any town.
4 All the trees could be very old or very young. It depends on the age of the street.
5 People without a car use other means of transport. Those at a railway station are going to use a train.

6 People who do not eat out are excluded.
7 Most people at an out-of-town shopping mall come by car.
8 People at an outpatients clinic are there because they have a health problem.
9 People who go to a gym go there to exercise.
10 People without a car who do not like reading.

Exam practice 2H

1 There are different ways of measuring shoe size.
2 It suggests the answer.
3 a People may lie.
  b 'Young' and 'old' mean different things to different people.
4 What methods did you use? Did you sit at a table? Did you do it quickly?
5 a means different things to different people.
  b What did you have for lunch yesterday? Snack, Full meal, did not eat.

Exam practice 3A

1 a 6   b Morocco
  c London   d 3 hr
2 a Bangkok   b 28 cm   c 12 cm
3 a 10   b 5   c 4th
  d Drive carefully. It is a dangerous spot.
4 a French   b History
  c 16   d 18
5 a 92
  b 
    Monday ✉✉✉✉
    Tuesday ✉✉✉◪
    Wednesday ✉✉✉✉✉✉
    Thursday ✉✉✉◪
    Friday ✉✉✉✉✉
6 a 16   b 42
  c
    Sport ☺☺☺☺
    Dancing ☺(
    Pop music ☺☺
    Other ☺☺☺

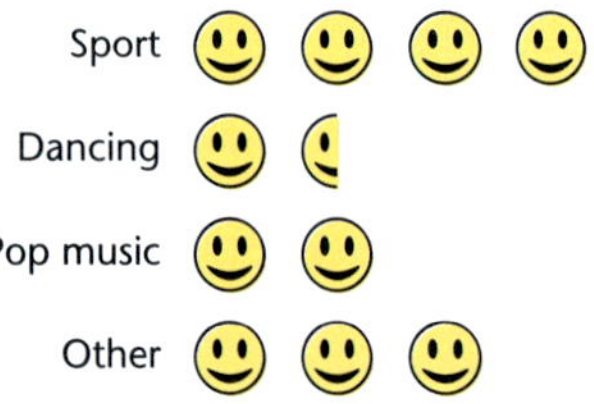

Exam practice 3B

1 a 8   b i 1   ii 1
  c 8   d 22   e 45
2 a 5   b Art
  c French   d 38
3 a cat   b 8   c 32
4 a Top Hill   b 10 000
  c i Crotton   ii 7500
5 a £2500   b £200
6 a C   b 17   c 4

Exam practice 3C

1

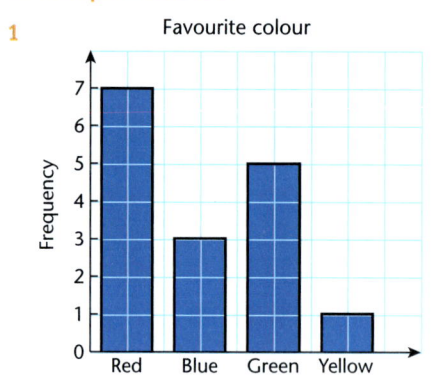

Favourite colour

(Bar chart: Red 7, Blue 3, Green 5, Yellow 1; y-axis: Frequency)

2 a 52
  b

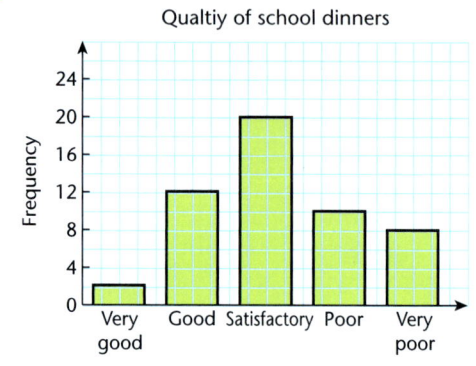

Qualtiy of school dinners

(Bar chart: Very good 2, Good 12, Satisfactory 20, Poor 10, Very poor 8; y-axis: Frequency)

3 a 45
  b football
  c

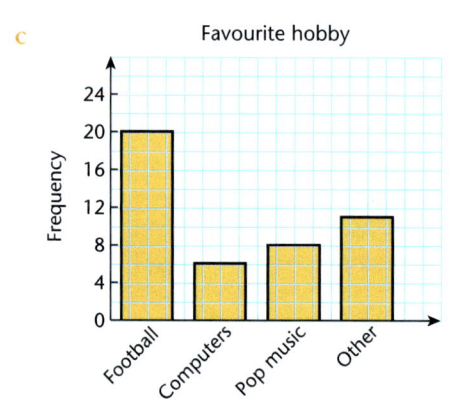

Favourite hobby

(Bar chart: Football 20, Computers 6, Pop music 8, Other 11; y-axis: Frequency)

4 a 30
  b

Geography grades

(Bar chart: A 4, B 8, C 11, D 5, E 2)

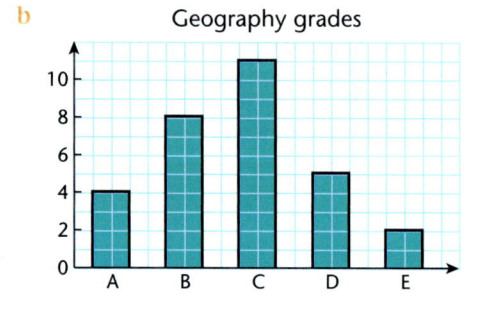

Answers 141

5 a 55 b car
  c *Vehicles passing the school gates* (bar chart: Bicycle 4, Motorbike 10, Car 25, Lorry 16)

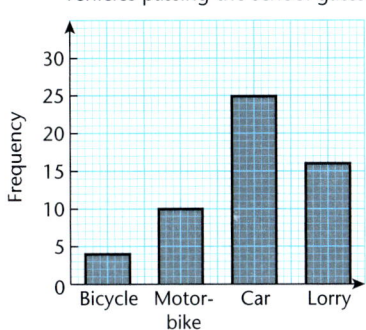

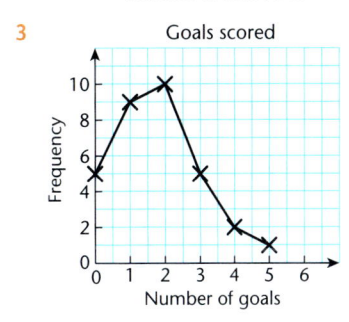

6 a 45
  b *Holidays abroad* (frequency polygon: 0→12, 1→18, 2→8, 3→4, 4→2, 5→1)

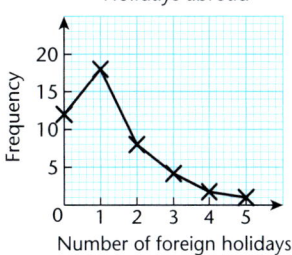

Exam practice 3D

1 a 18   b 10   c 14
2 *Number of bedrooms* (frequency polygon: 1→1, 2→5, 3→8, 4→4, 5→2)
3 *Goals scored* (frequency polygon: 0→5, 1→9, 2→10, 3→5, 4→2, 5→1)
4 *GCSE grades* (frequency polygon: 5→14, 6→18, 7→21, 8→12, 9→7, 10→5)
5 a 29
  b *Shoe sizes* (frequency polygon: 3→2, 3½→5, 4→10, 4½→8, 5→4)

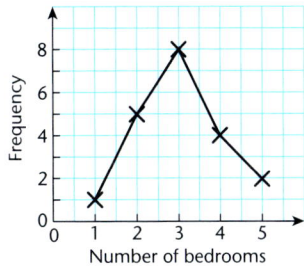

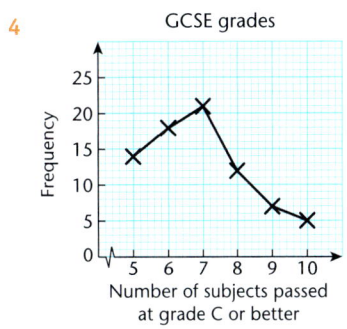

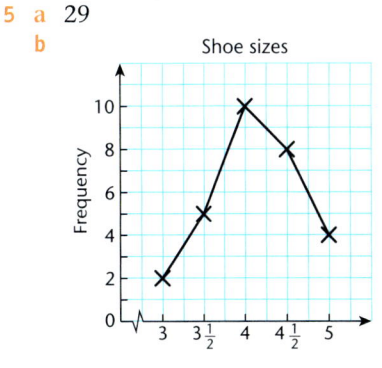

Exam practice 3E

1 a 30.5, 42.5, 54.5   b 82
  c *Number of passengers on buses* (frequency polygon: 5→21, 15→26, 25→14, 35→16, 45→16, 55→5)

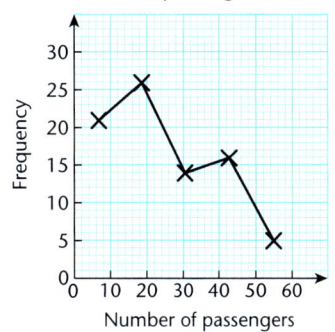

2 a 28, 33, 38, 43   b 31
  c *Number of competitors in a singing competition* (frequency polygon: 23→3, 28→2, 33→12, 38→9, 43→5)

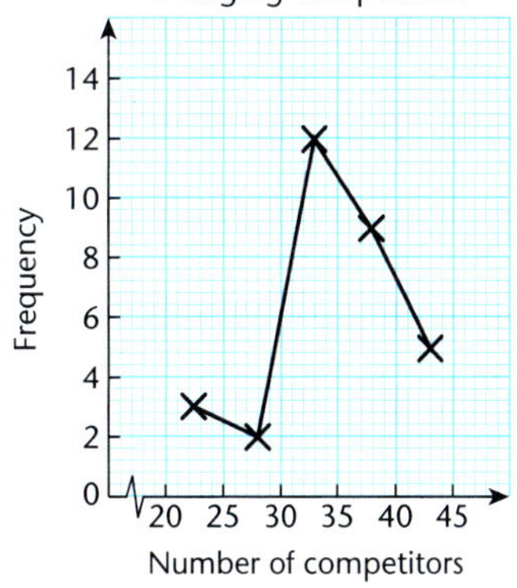

3 a missing values are 25, 35, 45, 55
  b *Times taken by a group of students to travel home one evening* (frequency polygon: 5→3, 15→10, 25→5, 35→4, 45→2, 55→1)

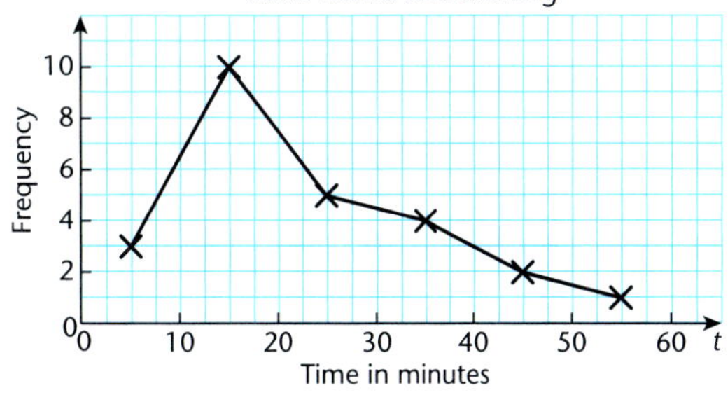

4 a missing values are 6, 8, 10, 12
   b Lengths of 50 pea pods (frequency polygon)

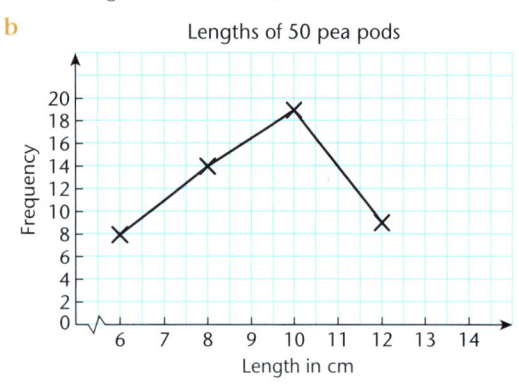

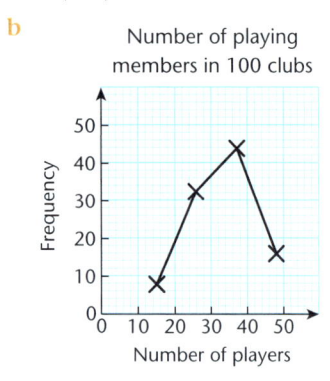

5 a 26, 37, 48
   b Number of playing members in 100 clubs (frequency polygon)

6 a missing values are 0.5, 1.5, 2.5, 3.5, 4.5
   b Heights of seedlings (frequency polygon)

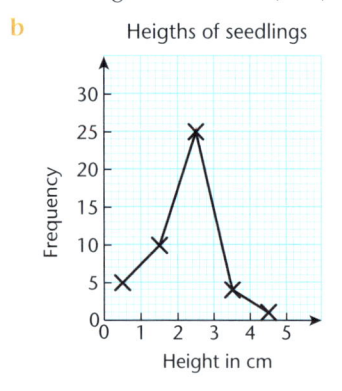

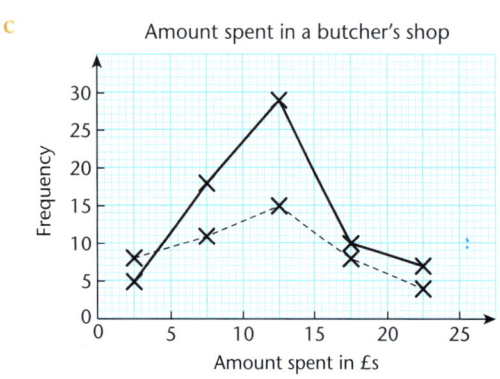

7 a 69   b 46
   c Amount spent in a butcher's shop (frequency polygon)

8 Time taken to complete a task (frequency polygon)

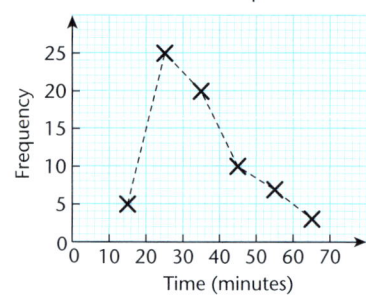

Exam practice 4A

1 a $\frac{1}{2}$ b £375
2 a Yes. The angle for Bennett is 90° which is $\frac{1}{4}$ of the circle.
   b 4800
3 a heating   b $\frac{1}{2}$ c hot water
4 a $\frac{1}{4}$ b 25
5 a 50   b $\frac{1}{3}$
6 a $\frac{1}{4}$ b 2500
   c Yes, more than half the circle is in the 21–60 group and half the population is 5000
7 a 72   b 54   c 6
8 a $\frac{1}{6}$ b £240
9 a No. The angle for children is 90° which is $\frac{1}{4}$ of the circle.
   b No. The angle for women is 150° which is bigger than the angle for men.

Exam practice 4B

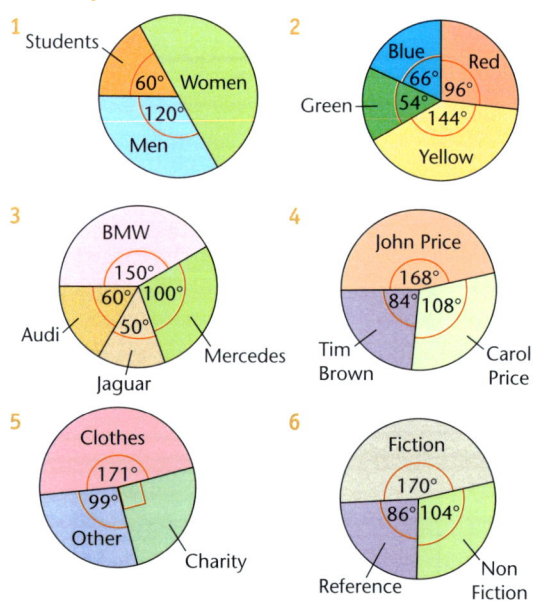

1 Students: Women 120°, Men, 60°
2 Blue 66°, Red 96°, Yellow 144°, Green 54°
3 BMW 150°, Mercedes 100°, Jaguar 50°, Audi 60°
4 John Price 168°, Carol Price 108°, Tim Brown 84°
5 Clothes 171°, Charity 99°, Other
6 Fiction 170°, Non Fiction 104°, Reference 86°

Exam practice 4C

1 a 15   b 93 g   c 5
2 a 26   b 47 sec
   c 12 sec   d 12
3 a 18   b 5 min 16 sec
   c 3   d 1 min 55 sec
4 a 15   b 10   c 5

Exam practice 4D

1 a 27   b 14
   c Marks
   ```
   1 | 4 4 5
   2 | 0 4 5 6 7 7 7 9
   3 | 0 0 1 2 3 3 4 4 4 4 4 4 5 5 6 8 9 9
   ```

2 a Time in minutes
   ```
   1 | 2 4 5 6 7 8 8 9 9
   2 | 0 0 1 1 5 7 7 9
   3 | 0 2 5
   ```
   b i 9   ii 13   iii 2

3 a 10
   b Price of books
   ```
   4 | 50 90 39 75
   5 | 40 70 95 80
   6 | 20 45
   ```
   c Price of books
   ```
   4 | 39 50 75 90
   5 | 40 70 80 95
   6 | 20 45
   ```

4 a 26
   b Number of minutes
   ```
   3 | 7 9
   4 | 1 7 5 2
   5 | 9 0 0 9 0 5 2 9 9
   6 | 1 6 0 1 5 8 1 8 9
   7 | 2 4
   ```
   c Number of minutes
   ```
   3 | 7 9
   4 | 1 2 5 7
   5 | 0 0 0 2 5 9 9 9 9
   6 | 0 1 1 1 5 6 8 8 9
   7 | 2 4
   ```
   d 10

5 a 12
   b Amount spent on lunch
   ```
   0 | 75 89
   1 | 56 90 86
   2 | 10 50 84 70 50 55 35
   ```
   c Amount spent on lunch
   ```
   0 | 75 89
   1 | 56 86 90
   2 | 10 35 50 50 55 70 84
   ```
   d 7

6 a 15
   b Number of calls
   ```
   0 | 9 7 6 4
   1 | 2 6 9 7 8 3 6
   2 | 8 5 1 4
   ```
   c Number of calls
   ```
   0 | 4 6 7 9
   1 | 2 3 6 6 7 8 9
   2 | 1 4 5 8
   ```
   d 11

Exam practice 4E

1 a i 38.8°C   ii midnight
   b 36.4°C   c 36.8°C   d 9 hr
   e Yes, 10 could have been correct (but she probably wasn't).

2 a i Nov.   ii May
   b Yes, Nov. and Dec. are the top two months of the year.

3 a i 39°C   ii 36°C
   b It could have been. The temperature is not plotted for 3.30 p.m.

4 a 250 p   b 390 p, 550 p, 530 p, 560 p, 590 p
   c Between year 3 and year 4.   d Price rises.

5 a i £975   ii May   b Dec.

6 a 60   b 65
   c Yes (115 is more than twice 45).

7 a & b   Annual rainfall in Blackwood 1995–2002

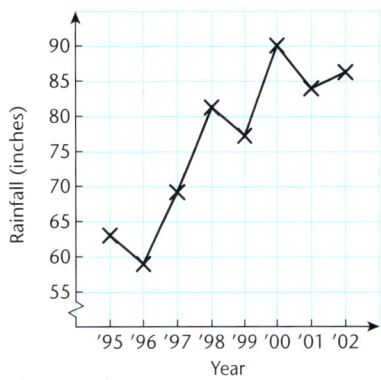

   c Yes, the trend is up.

8 a   Quarterly sales for toyshop

   b Yes for 01 and 02 but not for 03.

9 a   Number of students on roll at Durfield School

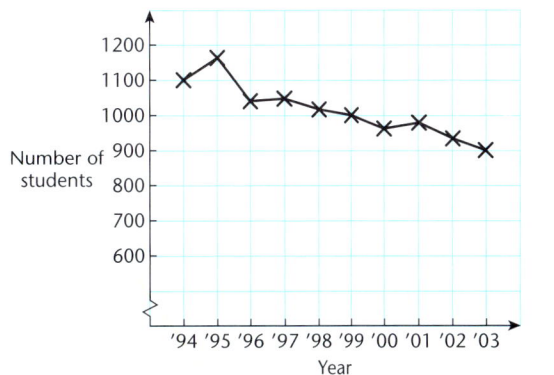

   b Yes. Since 1995 the number has fallen every year except 1997 and 2001.

Exam practice 4F

1 a Up   b 46%
2 Increased by 36%
3 a Less   b 5%, 95 is 5 lower than 100
4 145
5 80
6 a £250   b 50%   c 50

Exam practice 5A

1 a 4 marks   b 4 pets   c 10p
   d £7   e 3 yrs
2 a 0.8 cm   b 6 people c 24 g
   d 0.6 m   e 6 pencils

Exam practice 5B

1 a 12 yrs   b 9 sweets
   c 1.8 cm   d 56 pages
2 a 5.9 kg   b 26.4 cm
   c 155 cm   d 6.2 tonnes

Exam practice 5C

1 a 42 people b 17 people c 16 calls
   d 3.2 cm   e 5 min
2 a 12   b 98 cm
3 36 min
4 1.885 g
5 2
6 4

Exam practice 5D

1 a 6   b 35p
2 a £40   b £8
3 a 10 yrs   b 5 calls   c 15 chocolates
4 a 33 p   b 1.3 cm   c £17.28
5 a 5.3 cm   b 4.9 cm   c 5.14 cm

Exam practice 5E

1 a Heating   b Business and professional
   c Brown
2 a 4   b 3   c 3
3 a 3   b 33   c 34
4 a 4   b 1   c 1
5 a 22   b Saturday
6 a 14   b 2, 5 or 8 c $7\frac{1}{2}$
7 a 4   b 3   c $2\frac{1}{2}$
8 a 16   b 4   c 12
   d Jan–Mar
9 a 35   b 0   c 10
10 a 28   b 26   c 21

Exam practice 5F

1 a 8, 24, 12, 8   b 2
2 a 15   b 6, 10, 6, 8   c 2
3 a 30   b 0, 7, 32, 9 Total 48   c 1.6
4 a 0, 15, 12, 21, 8   b 40   c 1.4 cars
5 a 30   b £75   c £2.50

6 a

No. of kittens	Frequency	No. of kittens × frequency
0	2	0
1	1	1
2	2	4
3	4	12
4	6	24
5	2	10

   b 3
7 9 minutes
8 12

Exam practice 5G

1 a 200p   b 100p–149p   c 100p–149p
2 a £390 000   b £50 000–£99 000
   c £100 000 - £149 000
3 a 197   b £250
   c £251 - £300 d £201–£250
4 a 65   b 30
   c 6–10   d 6 - 10
5 a 250p   b 150p–199p   c 100p–149p
6 a 14   b 7–9   c 7–9
7 a 11   b 0–2   c 3–5

Exam practice 5H

1 53p
2 4 (nearest whole number)
3 19 min
4 7.6 cm
5 a 195
   b

Mid-interval value (minutes)	Frequency	Frequency × mid-interval value
2.5	25	62.5
7.5	35	262.5
12.5	80	1000
17.5	45	787.5
22.5	10	225
	Total: 195	Total: 2337.5

   c 12
6 a 20   b $5 \leq t < 10$
   c $5 \leq t < 10$ d 7.5 min
7 a 10 cm   b $154 \leq h < 156$
   c $152 \leq h < 154$ d 153.7 cm

Exam practice 6A

1 a 11   b 52
2 a 28   b 25   c 46
3 a 5   b 8   c 21
4 a 15   b 4   c 12
5 a 7   b 32
   c 105   d 118
6 a 73   b 3   c 45
7 a 55   b 53   c 12
8 a 32   b 18   c 12

Answers   145

Exam practice 6B

1 a 5   b 2
2 a 7   b 3
   c Yes, trend from graph is that as the age goes up the price goes down.
3 a No. The crosses are randomly distributed. They show no relationship.
   b 3
4 a B   b E   c 12
5 a

Houses and people

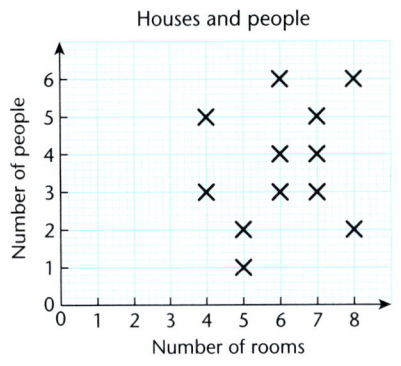

(scatter diagram: Number of rooms vs Number of people)

   b No, the relationship is fairly weak.
6 a

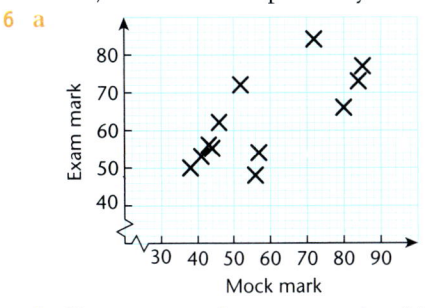

(scatter diagram: Mock mark vs Exam mark)

   b Yes, exam marks were mostly a bit higher than the mock marks
   c about 70

Exam practice 6C

1 18 hrs
2 a It is unlikely that the cross for the 5-yr old should be as far from the line of best fit as it is.
   b 900 g
3 a and b

Marks in French and Maths

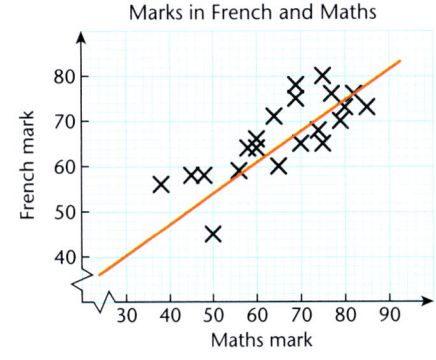

(scatter diagram: Maths mark vs French mark with line of best fit)

   c Moderate correlation i.e. high marks in maths tend to go with high marks in French.
   d Yes, students with high marks in French tend to get high marks in maths.
   e 67 (± 2)

Exam practice 6D

1 a and b

Weight and height of 10 people

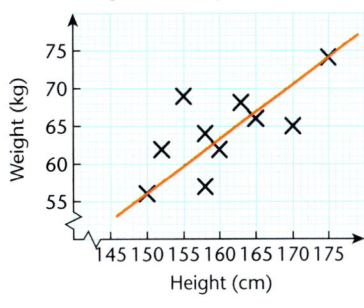

(scatter diagram: Height (cm) vs Weight (kg) with line of best fit)

   c Tall people tend to weigh more than short people, i.e. moderate correlation.

2 a and b

People and rooms

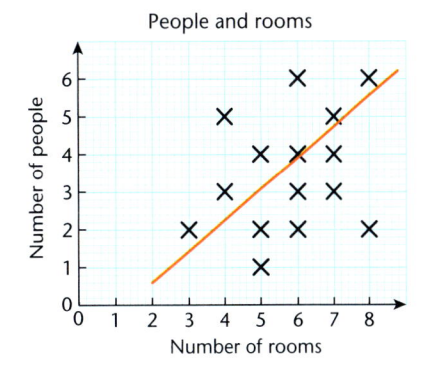

(scatter diagram: Number of rooms vs Number of people with line of best fit)

   c Weak positive correlation.
   d 10 (± 2)
   e Not particularly reliable. The estimate is off the graph and the correlation is not very strong.
   f Two pieces of information to go in each box in the bottom row. This can lead to confusion.

3 a

Textbooks, pens and pencils

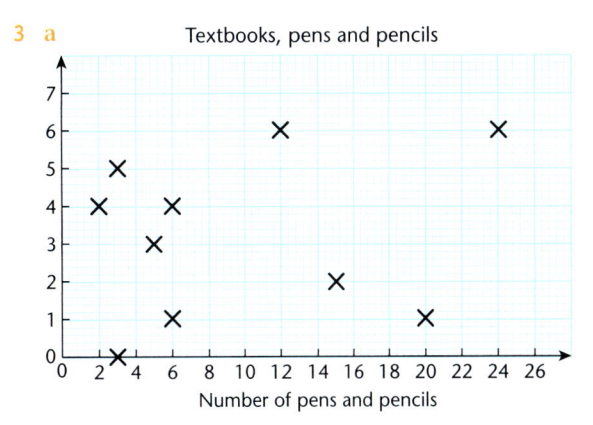

(scatter diagram: Number of pens and pencils vs textbooks)

   b The scatter diagram shows no pattern. The crosses look randomly placed.
   c Need to define what a book is. Is it a text book, an exercise book or what?

4 a A, B or C   b B or C
   c B or C   d D
   e A   f B or C

5 a

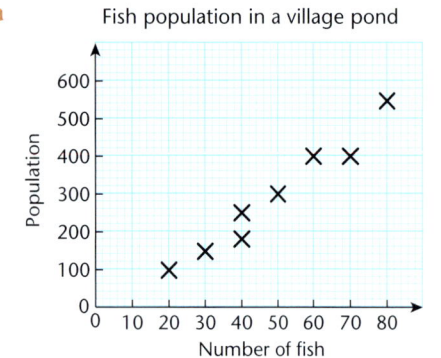

Fish population in a village pond

b The points are very close to a line but this does not mean that increasing the number of fish will increase the population.

Exam practice 7A

1. H, T
2. 1,2,3,4
3. red disc, blue disc, yellow disc
4. 1,2,3,4,5,6,7,8,9,10
5. red crayon, yellow crayon, blue crayon, brown crayon, black crayon, green crayon.
6. packet of chewing gum, packet of boiled sweets, bar of chocolate.
7. 2p, 5p, 20p, 50p
8. a 5   b 2, 3, 5, 7, 11
9. 2,4,6,8,10
10. 52

Exam practice 7B

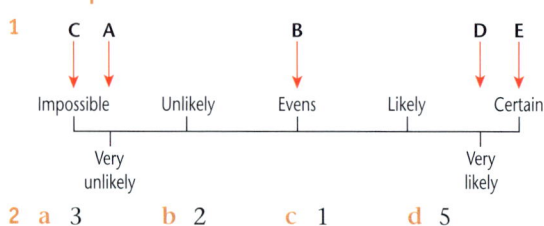

1. C, A, B, D, E on scale Impossible — Very unlikely — Unlikely — Evens — Likely — Very likely — Certain
2. a 3   b 2   c 1   d 5
3. Yes, there are 2 discs, one of each colour so the chance that one of them is chosen is evens.
4. Yes, a *fair* dice means that every number is equally likely.
5. No, a red disc is twice as likely as blue disc.
6. Yes, half the discs are green.

Exam practice 7C

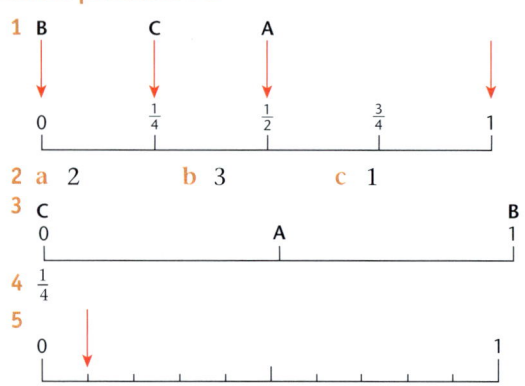

1. B at 0, C at $\frac{1}{4}$, A at $\frac{1}{2}$, arrow at 1
2. a 2   b 3   c 1
3. C at 0, A at middle, B at 1
4. $\frac{1}{4}$
5. arrow near 0

6. $\frac{1}{3}$
7. $\frac{1}{5}$
8. $\frac{1}{7}$
9. $\frac{1}{400}$
10. 1
11. 0

Exam practice 7D

1. a 6   b $\frac{1}{3}$
2. $\frac{1}{5}$
3. $\frac{3}{5}$
4. $\frac{2}{5}$
5. a 4   b $\frac{4}{9}$
6. a 10   b $\frac{1}{2}$
7. a 52   b i $\frac{1}{13}$ ii $\frac{1}{2}$ iii $\frac{1}{4}$
8. a $\frac{3}{10}$ b $\frac{1}{5}$ c $\frac{3}{10}$ d $\frac{1}{5}$
9. a $\frac{1}{2}$ b $\frac{2}{3}$ c $\frac{1}{3}$
10. 0 — C, A, B on scale to 1
11. A, B, C on scale 0 to 1
12. a 3   b 2   c 4   d 1
13. a $\frac{1}{4}$ b $\frac{1}{40}$
14. a $\frac{1}{3}$
    b Doesn't say how many boys and girls there are!

Exam practice 7E

1. $\frac{1}{2}$
2. a 20   b $\frac{4}{5}$
3. $\frac{2}{7}$
4. 46, $\frac{5}{23}$
5. $\frac{8}{15}$

Exam practice 7F

1. about 50
2. 10
3. 20
4. a 10   b 20
5. 20
6. a 15   b 45   c 30
7. 20
8. 10
9. 10
10. 5
11. 25
12. a $\frac{1}{2}$ b 30
    c No, possible but not certain.
    d Probably, you'd expect about 50.

Answers

Exam practice 7G
1. a £10 b 5 c £5
   d Lose, spending greater than likely winnings.
2. a 2 b £50
   c Spends £50 more than winnings.
3. a 2 b £20, £25.60
   d No, she spends £25.60, likely to win £20.
4. Yes. Likely loss £48, likely win £52

Exam practice 8A
1. 0.1
2. a $\frac{1}{10}$ b $\frac{9}{10}$
3. 0.18
4. 0.32
5. a $\frac{2}{5}$ b $\frac{3}{5}$
6. $\frac{24}{25}$
7. $\frac{97}{100}$
8. 0.3
9. $\frac{3}{5}$
10. 0.4

Exam practice 8B
1. 0.4
2. $\frac{1}{5}$
3. $\frac{1}{3}$
4. a 0.2
   b Purple, it has the greatest probability.
5. a 0.6 b 40
6. a 0.3 b 15
7. 0.1
8. 0.2
9. a 0.25
   b Yes. The probability Anna wins (0.25) is the same as the probability that Erin wins.
10. a 0.82
    b Will arrive on time – this is the greatest probability.

Exam practice 8C

1.
Coin	Spinner		
	2	4	6
H	H, 2	H, 4	H, 6
T	T, 2	T, 4	T, 6

2.
Coin	Dice					
	1	2	3	4	5	6
H	H, 1	H, 2	H, 3	H, 4	H, 5	H, 6
T	T, 1	T, 2	T, 3	T, 4	T, 5	T, 6

3.
2nd spin	1st spin		
	1	2	3
1	1, 1	1, 2	1, 3
2	2, 1	2, 2	2, 3
3	3, 1	3, 2	3, 3

4.
Disc	Spinner		
	1	2	3
1	1, 1	1, 2	1, 3
2	2, 1	2, 2	2, 3

Disc	Spinner		
	1	2	3
1	2	3	4
2	3	4	5

5.
Three sided Spinner	Four-sided Spinner			
	1	2	3	4
1	2	3	4	5
2	3	4	5	6
3	4	5	6	7

6. a 6 b 1

7.
10p coin	Dice					
	1	2	3	4	5	6
H	2	4	6	8	10	12
T	1	2	3	4	5	6

Exam practice 8D
1. a $\frac{2}{9}$ b $\frac{2}{3}$
2. a $\frac{1}{6}$ b $\frac{7}{12}$
3. a
Spinner	Dice					
	1	2	3	4	5	6
1	1, 1	1, 2	1, 3	1, 4	1, 5	1, 6
2	2, 1	2, 2	2, 3	2, 4	2, 5	2, 6
3	3, 1	3, 2	3, 3	3, 4	3, 5	3, 6

b $\frac{1}{6}$

4. a
Spinner	Dice					
	1	2	3	4	5	6
1	2	3	4	5	6	7
2	3	4	5	6	7	8
3	4	5	6	7	8	9

b $\frac{2}{3}$

5. a
2nd Bag	1st Bag				
	10p	10p	10p	50p	50p
10p	10p 10p	10p 10p	10p 10p	10p 50p	10p 50p
50p	50p 10p	50p 10p	50p 10p	50p 50p	50p 50p

b i $\frac{3}{10}$ ii $\frac{1}{2}$

6 a

	1st dice					
	1	2	3	4	5	6
1	1,1	1,2	1,3	1,4	1,5	1,6
2	2,1	2,2	2,3	2,4	2,5	2,6
3	3,1	3,2	3,3	3,4	3,5	3,6
4	4,1	4,2	4,3	4,4	4,5	4,6
5	5,1	5,2	5,3	5,4	5,5	5,6
6	6,1	6,2	6,3	6,4	6,5	6,6

(2nd dice)

b i $\frac{1}{6}$ ii $\frac{1}{6}$ c about 2

7 a

Coin	Spinner		
	1	2	3
H	3	6	9
T	1	2	3

b $\frac{1}{6}$
c i £2 ii Lose, cost £6, likely winnings £2.

8 $\frac{1}{4}$

9 $\frac{1}{36}$

Exam practice 8E

1 a $\frac{3}{20}$ b $\frac{1}{6}$ c $\frac{1}{6}$
 d Yes, actual number is the same as estimated number.
2 a $\frac{1}{5}$ b $\frac{2}{5}$ c $\frac{3}{10}$
 d Yes, probability is 0.29; actual value is 0.3 i.e. almost the same.
3 a $\frac{7}{10}$ b 7
4 a $\frac{5}{12}$ b about 14600 (nearest 100)
5 a $\frac{1}{25}$ b 8
6 a $\frac{33}{100}$ b 33
7 a $\frac{4}{7}$ b $\frac{2}{5}$
8 a 94 b $\frac{6}{25}$ c 2500
9 a Quite possibly; the estimated probability of choosing a green sweet is $\frac{50}{200} = \frac{1}{4}$
 There are 200 sweets in the bag so the number of green sweets expected is $200 \times \frac{1}{4} = 50$.
 b $\frac{3}{4}$

Exam practice 9A

These answers are 'for example'. There is no one correct answer.

1 It is only a sample. It could be biased
2 There must always be values above and below the average unless they are all the same.
3 Probably not. Do not know which average was used - mean, mode or median.
4 a 9
 b Mode or median
5 a 40 b $\frac{1}{8}$
 c 1000. He only weighed some of the tomatoes.

6 No: 10 get less than £6/hr and 10 get £6 or more per hr.
7 a £10 000 b £10 000 c £14 625
 d £10 000, it's the mode and the median. More people earn this than anything else.
8 a $\frac{1}{10}$ b 2000
 c The proportion without a car is based on a sample of 100 people. The sample may not be representative.
9 a $\frac{2}{5}$
 b No, the data is for a sample of 100 students not 3000.
10 The trend (3% down to 2.2%) over six months shows downward movement. Gordon has assumed that the trend will continue down.
11 No; there is not a strong relationship between the number of children and the number of pets.
12 There is a fairly strong relationship for these 7 people but the sample is much too small to make such a statement.

Exam practice 9B

1 a South West
 b Yes. Green fraction in South West is about half that in the North East.
2 The City authority spends a much higher proportion than the County authority on education. The Country authority spends a higher proportion than the city authority on 'other services'.
3 a Sydney b 24 cm
 c No. More in New York Oct–Dec. than in Sydney.
4 a July–Sept. b Jan–March
 c 11°C d April–June.
5 a 11 b 11 c 11
 d On each day of the second week more are absent than the corresponding day the first week.
6 Fewer under 16 in 2005 than in 1995. Far more over 65 in 2005 than in 1995.
7 More sunshine in Sandown than St Andrew's every month except June. The difference is greater in the fourth quarter of the year than the first quarter.
8 Grades in maths tend to be lower than for English. There is a greater spread in maths than in English.
9 a 1 min 28 sec. b 1 min 35 sec.
 c Bigger range for females than males. Faster average times for males than females.
10 a 10 b 19
 c There are more words per sentence on average in the book than in the newspaper.
 d Not necessarily. This statement is based on one paragraph from one book and one page from one newspaper.

11 The estimates for the length of line A tend to be less than the estimates for the length of line B.
    People tend to underestimate the length of line A and overestimate the length of line B. This is probably because of an optical illusion.

12 [Graph: Marks for science test, Number of students vs Mark]

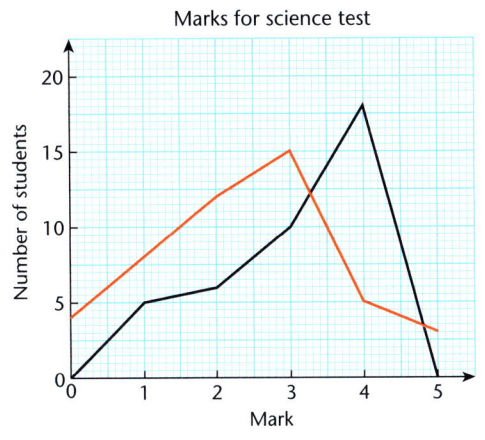

  b Bigger range for Group B than Group A. Modal mark for Group A is higher than the modal mark for Group B.

13 a Line 1   b Line 2   c 46
   d Line 2 produced fewer defective radios on Monday and Tuesday.

Examination practice paper
Section A
1 a red   b 58   c 6   d 136
2 a C, A, B   b i $0.7 + 0.2 + 0.2 > 1$ ii 0
3 a i $70° + 115° + 35° + 140° = 360°$ ii 420
   b 10
4 a   4 | 2 6 2 9
       5 | 6 9
       6 | 5 1
       7 | 7 0
   b 35

5
Number of minutes, t	Frequency	Midpoint
$0 < t \leq 4$	10	2
$4 < t \leq 8$	20	4
$8 < t \leq 12$	12	6
$12 < t \leq 16$	8	10

7.44 minutes

Section B
1 a
Type of pet	Tally	Frequency
Dog	||||‌ |||	8
Hamster	||||	4
Cat	||||‌		6
Rabbit	||	2

  b
Dog	◯ ◯
Hamster	◯
Cat	◯ ◖
Rabbit	◖

  c rabbit, hamster, cat, dog

2 a Wednesday   b 300   c 385

3 a
	Spinner A		
	1	3	5
2	3	5	7
4	5	7	9
6	7	9	11

Spinner B

   b i 1   ii $\frac{2}{3}$

4 a i and ii

[Scatter graph: Temperature (°C) vs Number of drinks sold]

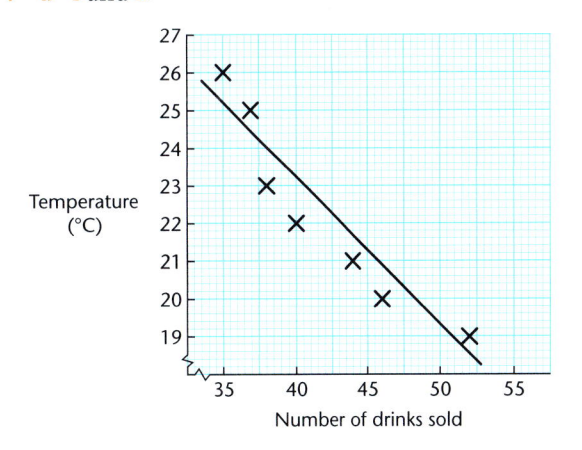

   iii 22.4° (± 0.2)   iv negative correlation
   b There is no linear correlation between X and Y.

Index

A
arithmetic mean 59
average
   misunderstanding 116–17
   most commonly used 59
   summary of key points 74

B
bar charts 26, 29, 121
biased 18, 89

C
census 4, 18
chance 88–9
class intervals 14, 67
collecting data, summary of key points 22
compound event 105–6
continuous data 13–14
correlation 82–3

D
data
   class intervals 14
   collection sheets 8–10
   continuous 13–14
   discrete 13–14
   estimate for population 116–17
   index numbers 52
   primary 2–3
   qualitative 7
   quantitative 7, 13
   related 16–17
   sampling 18
   secondary 2–3
   time-series 48
   two-way table 16–17
   ungrouped 26, 30–1, 64–5
data collection, summary of key points 22
data conclusions, summary of key points 127
   data, grouped
   definition 11
   frequency polygon 33
   mean 70–1
   median 67–8
   mode 67–8
   range 67–8
   two-way table 17
data representation, summaries of key points 37, 54
discrete data 13–14
dual charts 121
dual frequency polygon 125

E
equally likely 88–9
estimated range 68
evens 88–9
event
   certain 90
   compound 105–6
   definition 87
   estimating frequency 96–7
   impossible 90
   multiple happenings 92
   not happening 101
experiment 87

F
fair 89
frequency 8
frequency diagrams 95
frequency distribution 70–1
frequency polygon
   grouped data 33
   ungrouped data 30–1
frequency scale 26
frequency table 8, 26, 30–1, 60–1
   grouped data 67–8
   ungrouped data 64–5

G
games of chance 98
grouped data
   definition 11
   frequency polygon 33
   mean 70–1
   median 67–8
   mode 67–8

range 67–8
two-way table 17
grouped frequency table 33

H
handling data cycle 1
hypothesis 1–2

I
index numbers 52

L
leading questions 20
line of best fit 80
linear correlation 82–3

M
manageability 4
mean 59, 64–5, 70–1
median 57–8, 60–1, 67–8
mid-interval value 33
modal group 68
mode 56, 60–1, 67–8
mutually exclusive outcomes 103

N
National Census 18
negative linear correlation 82–3
Nightingale, Florence 1
no linear correlation 83
notation
   less than (<) 14
   less than or equal to (≤) 14

O
open ended questions 20
outcome 103

P
pictograms 23
pie charts 38, 41
positive linear correlation 82–3
primary data 2–3
probability
   calculating 90
   certain event 90
   chance 88–9
   compound event 105–6
   definition 87
   equally likely 88–9
   evens 88–9
   using a sample space 108
   games of chance 98
   impossible event 90
   multiple happenings of an event 92
   mutually exclusive outcomes 103
   number of times an event happens 96–7
   outcome 87, 103
   relative frequency 111
   sample spaces 105–6, 108
   scale 88–9
   summaries of key points 100, 115
probability, event
   certainty 90
   compound 105–6
   definition 87
   estimating frequency 96–7
   impossible 90
   multiple happenings 92
   not happening 101

Q
qualitative data 7
quantitative data 7, 13
questionnaire 19–20
questionnaire assumptions 117

R
random 90
range 55, 60–1, 67–8
   summary of key points 74
related data 16–17
relative frequency 111
representative sample 18
representing data, summaries of key points 37, 54
response 19–20

S
sample 4, 18, 116–17
sample spaces 105–6, 108
scatter graphs 77–8
   summary of key points 86
secondary data 2–3
statistical investigation, summary of key points 6
stem plot 43
stem-and-leaf diagrams 43–4, 45
strong linear correlation 82–3
survey 4, 18, 116–17
survey assumptions 117

T
tally mark 8
task manageability 4
time–series graphs 48
trial 111
two-way tables 16–17, 75
   summary of key points 86

U
unbiased 89
ungrouped data 26, 30–1, 64–5
unrepresentative sample 18

W
weak linear correlation 83